I0881404

Painting

Wargaming Figures

AXIS FORCES ON THE EASTERN FRONT

Painting Wargaming Figures
AXIS FORCES ON THE EASTERN FRONT

Andy Singleton

Pen & Sword
MILITARY
AN IMPRINT OF PEN & SWORD BOOKS LTD.
YORKSHIRE – PHILADELPHIA

First published in Great Britain in 2021 by
Pen & Sword Military
An imprint of
Pen & Sword Books Ltd
Yorkshire – Philadelphia

ISBN 978 1 52676 560 4

A CIP catalogue record for this book is available from the British Library.

Typeset in Gill Sans 12/16 by SJmagic DESIGN SERVICES, India.
Printed and bound in India by Replika Press Pvt. Ltd.

Pen & Sword Books Limited incorporates the imprints of Atlas, Archaeology, Aviation, Discovery, Family History, Fiction, History, Maritime, Military, Military Classics, Politics, Select, Transport, True Crime, Air World, Frontline Publishing, Leo Cooper, Remember When, Seaforth Publishing, The Praetorian Press, Wharncliffe Local History, Wharncliffe Transport, Wharncliffe True Crime and White Owl.

For a complete list of Pen & Sword titles please contact

PEN & SWORD BOOKS LIMITED
47 Church Street, Barnsley, South Yorkshire, S70 2AS, England
E-mail: enquiries@pen-and-sword.co.uk
Website: www.pen-and-sword.co.uk

Or
PEN AND SWORD BOOKS
1950 Lawrence Rd, Havertown, PA 19083, USA
E-mail: Uspen-and-sword@casematepublishers.com
Website: www.penandswordbooks.com

MIX
Paper from responsible sources
FSC www.fsc.org FSC® C016779

Contents

Introduction

When Operation BARBAROSSA began in 1941, it heralded the start of one of the most apocalyptic conflicts in history. Four years of war would see millions dead, and vast swathes of cities and land destroyed. The fighting stretched from frozen plains to parched, dusty plains over thousands of miles. Battles were fought with thousands of personnel and tanks clashing in barely comprehensible numbers.

Within such a vast theatre of war, the range of uniforms and equipment was also huge. Just in terms of field uniforms, Germany had a different pattern for almost every year of the war and numerous camouflage uniforms. Coupled with their co-belligerent powers, the modelling scope is quite vast and somewhat hard to comprehend; hopefully, this book will assist in adding some clarity to the confusing array of equipment issued.

This period saw the rapid evolution of personal camouflage clothing. The various patterns used are all complex and daunting to paint, with subtle minutiae between the changing variants and patterns. I've broken these down into clean, simple guides that should make it easier to replicate using a simple process.

A bewildering array of equipment was used on the Eastern Front. It is impossible to cover every combination and permutation of dye and manufacturing periods in a volume of this size; however, I have attempted to cover all the basic and most common combinations. I've also attempted to cover the issue and usage dates of various equipment. I haven't gone into too much detail on insignia and field gear as those would take a volume of their own to describe.

One way of adding a more interesting element to your Eastern Front wargaming is to add the forces of one or more of the Axis powers.

While often overlooked in favour of the large armoured clashes of famous German divisions, the Axis forces shouldered a significant burden of the fighting in Russia in operations that are well suited to gaming.

Finally, I hope that this book helps to make putting your collections together easier and motivates you to get them painted and onto the table!

1

Tools: Basic tools and modelling advice

TIPS AND TOOLS

Getting started

One of the major issues facing the forces of the Axis was the huge and bewildering array of matériel in use. Equipment was drawn from across the length and breadth of Europe, requiring an equally huge and disparate logistical system. In some ways this is reflected today, as someone first entering into collecting and modelling the campaigns in Eastern Europe is presented with an overwhelming array of models, scales, paints, glues and tools, as well as a vast number of other elements.

While the huge range of hobby products, paints and tools on the market is truly vast and expanding rapidly all the time, this book will attempt to provide some guidance and knowledge on the most commonly-required tools and techniques. I'll also attempt to cut through some of the technical terminology, giving a bite-size description of what is required for a few of the most commonly-used techniques.

As a solid rule of thumb, when it comes to buying tools you're better off buying better quality. These may prove more expensive, but will work out cheaper in the long run and the results will be more than worth it. That said, it's probably also worth scouring the internet and checking with club mates or friends for reviews to see if it sounds like something you would find useful and fulfils your specific tastes and needs.

Readers of the other books in this series will be familiar with the following sections; however, I've repeated it here for those new to the hobby.

Plastic, metal or resin?

The Second World War is probably the most widely-supported period for models in any and all scales, with thousands of different products available. Generally speaking, for gaming purposes these are provided in either white metal, resin or hard and soft plastics.

Plastic figures are typically provided on a frame called a sprue, from which they need to be removed. Since about the 1960s, many extremely popular and classic sets of figures from the likes of Airfix, Esci and Revell have been produced, predominantly 20mm-sized figures produced in a soft, polythene type of plastic that required a vigorous scrubbing with warm water and washing-up liquid before painting. Thankfully, this is becoming less prevalent and modern miniatures, typically being produced in hard plastic which is far less prone to warping and bending, has better adhesion for paint and is also far easier to glue. The 28mm-sized figures are most commonly a hard plastic, though there are also several hard plastic 15mm and 20mm ranges. The majority of 28mm figure manufacturers provide each figure in several pieces to allow you

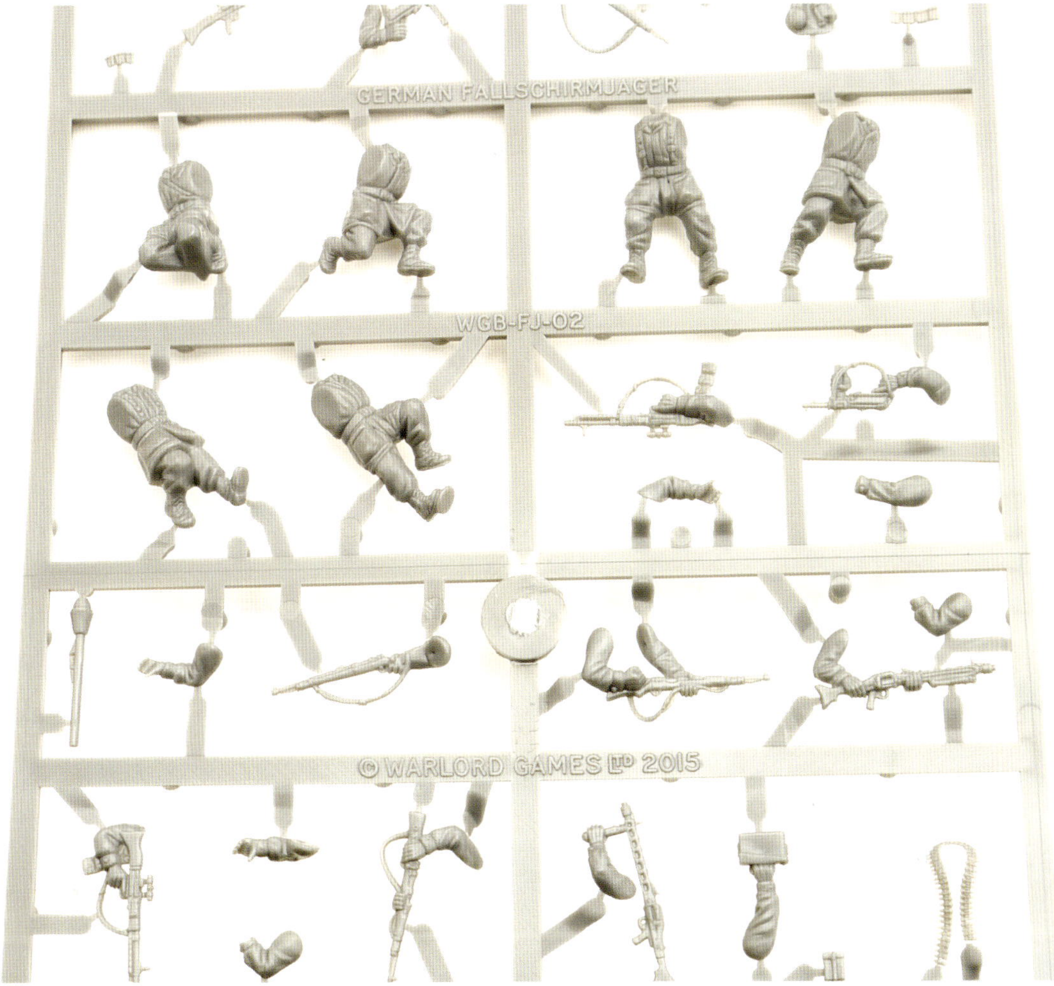

some variety in their posing, and I'll go into more detail in assembling these a little later. Plastic figures are best assembled with special-purpose plastic glues, again something I'll discuss later.

Probably the most common material for the production of wargames figures, however, is lead-free metal, and these figures dominate all the various gaming scales. Most historical ranges are produced in this material, and the figures are usually supplied as single-piece castings and typically come with a small stand attached to the figures' feet to aid placing them on their bases. Both plastic and metal figures can have moulding lines along their sides, and occasionally excess areas of metal or plastic called

flash as a by-product of the production process that will need to be removed. This is a simple task and requires scraping along the line with the blunt side of a blade or a quick sanding down with some files. Again, I'll cover that a little later too.

Metal models require assembling with superglue or an equivalent, and larger models such as artillery and cavalry will require a degree of patience as they can quickly become somewhat frustrating if you try to rush putting them together. When assembling any figure, though, patience and test-fitting will always pay off here.

Relatively rare, although some ranges are starting to introduce it as a material, is resin. This is at first glance much like plastic, though is a little more brittle and is often supplied with casting blocks that need trimming away. Resin is light with crisp detail and is best treated as working with metal, using superglue for assembly.

KNIVES, CUTTERS AND FILES

The first thing you'll need to do, unsurprisingly, is to get the component parts of your figure ready for assembly and clean away any residue from the manufacturing process. This can take several forms, but the most common are flash and mould lines which form when the model is being cast in its mould. These appear as either prominent lines around a figure or as chunks or 'worms' of excess material, most especially on edges and undercuts of the figure. These casting imperfections can appear in any material and removing them will massively improve the appearance of the finished model, especially when you are using the dry brush techniques.

Hobby knife

These broadly fall into two types: those with replaceable blades such as the ubiquitous X-Acto hobby knife, and the Stanley knife. Either one of these will probably be your most frequently used tool in preparing your figures, as the sharp side of the blade can be used for cutting things while the blunt edge can be used to remove mould lines by simply scraping it down them a few times. This works, as the blunt edge is more forgiving of slips and follows the contours of the details well.

Which type of knife you get is entirely up to you, but I'd recommend one of each, especially as they can be found pretty much anywhere that sells tools or hobby supplies at good prices. The replaceable blades of the X-Acto style allow different styles and shapes of blade to be fitted, as well as allowing you to simply replace the blade once it becomes dull. The slender, sharp blades do have their limits, however, and can blunt quickly when working with metal and may also struggle with cutting through thicker plastic sprues. They are very sharp, though, and give you a lot of control, especially for scraping off moulding lines or the remains of tabs after using side cutters. The Stanley knife is handy if you need to do some heavier-duty cutting, such as trimming parts off for a conversion that side cutters can't perform as cleanly as you need.

Side cutters

Also known as sprue cutters, these are vaguely similar to scissors but with a shorter blade and more powerful tensioned action. As the name suggests,

Affix stamp here

Pen and Sword Books
c/o Casemate Publishers
1950 Lawrence Road
Havertown, PA 19083

these are good at cutting things. Perfect for removing plastic parts from their carrying sprue, it's best to trim the part leaving a small stub of plastic that you can then trim with a knife or file. Also handy for metal, these can also be used for removing casting lugs or parts from moulding blocks. Sprue cutters can be found in the majority of model shops, both on and offline. I'd recommend getting maybe two sets and having one for metal and one for plastic if you're likely to work on a lot of both materials, as the set for metal will blunt faster than the set used on plastics.

Files

Files are another immensely useful tool, and can be found in most tool/ hardware shops, as well as in model and hobby shops. Ideally, what you want is a set of jeweller's files or needle files. These typically come in sets of several different files, with each being a different shape to allow the cleaning of most parts of a model. A file with a blade more than a centimetre wide will probably prove to be too big for modelling purposes, so aim for something quite fine. These are great tools for removing mould lines and getting rid of the contact points of sprue gates.

GLUES

Now that we have established what the figures are made from and have trimmed and cleaned the parts, it's time to start sticking things together. For this, we'll need to ensure that we are matching the correct bonding agent to the right material. Very broadly speaking, the most commonly encountered glues are PVA, superglue, cement and solvent. PVA is a sticky paste and fine for attaching the basing materials to your figures' bases but is pretty useless for actually sticking your figures together.

Superglue, or cyanoacrylate to give it its proper name, is a rapid-curing cement that bonds most materials. Given the rapidity of the bonding process, superglue works best when used in small controlled areas. I tend to apply it with a cocktail stick or something similar, and apply

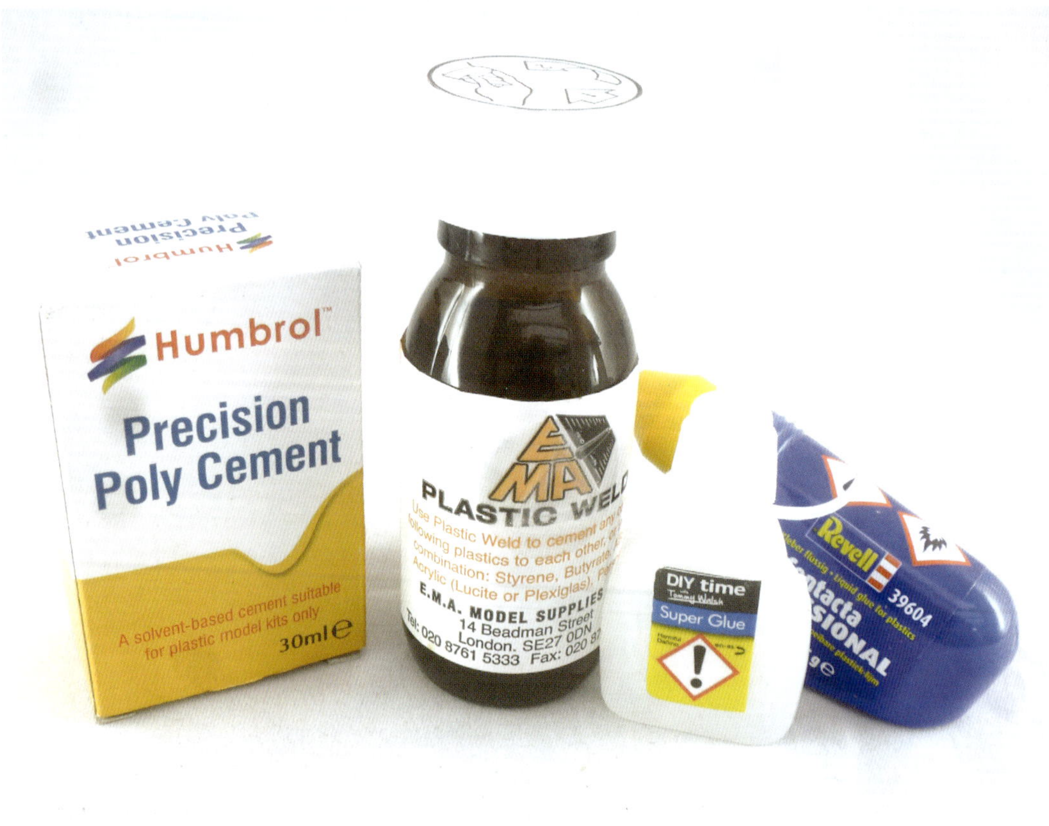

small dabs to each part that will be bonded. It's better to get the parts joined and then come back and carefully add more superglue if you feel the bond needs it rather than flooding an area that will take forever to dry and potentially make a terrible mess of your model too.

Adhesives for plastics such as those from Revell, Tamiya and Humbrol are all solvent-based to varying degrees and have a fairly wide range of drying times. In addition, there are also solvents designed with modelling in mind, such as Plastic Weld, which are far more potent products. All of these, however, function on the basis of partially melting the two bonding surfaces of plastic into a very strong bond. They won't, however, bond metal, resin or plastic to metal or resin. For this you will still need superglue.

Finally, we have cements. These typically come supplied in tubes and are very sticky and foul-smelling. While eventually they can give a decent bond, they are for the most part quite inferior to the purpose-designed adhesives already mentioned and should probably be avoided.

It's also worth checking the drying times for various glues. Superglue can have an activator that will speed up the drying times for when you need an even quicker bond. Alternatively, especially when working with small parts, a more gel-type glue is very good as this will hold the part in place and also allow you to adjust positioning and fit. It's also handy when assembling figures as it gives you some time to play around with poses.

FILLER

When assembling multi-part models, it is perhaps inevitable that some gaps or joins may not look as natural as we would like. This can result from a number of causes, such as ill-fitting parts, multi-pose sets being positioned beyond their designer's original intent or even conversions where parts have been cut and repositioned, to name but three possible examples. Perhaps the most prevalent of these, though, is the seam between arm and shoulder or wrist and arm. Sometimes these can be hidden or cleaned up using files as described earlier, but other times the join will be too big or too prominent to hide. Now when you're putting together a few hundred figures or building a full battalion of figures for a club or show game, these niceties may not be high on your list of priorities in terms of finishing the figures. The process can be quite time-consuming, so whether it's worth doing depends on the value to you of the additional time investment.

If you do decide to fill the seams and gaps, then broadly speaking there are two types of filler you can use: epoxy putty and model filler. The key distinction between these is that filler comes pre-mixed, ready to apply usually in a tube not too dissimilar to toothpaste, and epoxy putty is made by mixing two compounds together.

Model filler is pretty easy to find in most brick-and-mortar hobby shops, and is widely manufactured by the likes of Humbrol, Revell, Vallejo and the like. Filler is very easy to use: simply squeeze a bit of filler onto some card and then apply the filler to the necessary area with a cocktail stick. Once dry, it's easily sanded with files or wet and dry paper. Most fillers take a few hours to dry before they are ready to be sanded and shaped.

Epoxy putty, most recognizably Milliput or Green Stuff, though there are others, is supplied as two essentially clay-like compounds and these are mixed together in equal parts. Generally these will be in two contrasting colours, and when mixing them the idea is to create one consistent solid colour. Green Stuff, for example, is provided as a yellow and blue ribbon that when mixed makes green. Once mixed, epoxy putty can be applied to the model in the same way as model filler, applying it neatly to the gap.

While epoxy putty needs slightly more preparation work, it does have the advantage of being easy to shape and sculpt. This allows it to be pushed and blended into the area needing to be filled by simply keeping your tools wet and working it until you achieve the desired result. This then serves to minimize the amount of filling and sanding needed to finish the piece.

One other benefit of using epoxy putty is that it lasts a very long time without being mixed. I've had several tubes of differing types that

lasted several years and were still good to use. Price-wise, both types of filler tend to be broadly similar. The modelling fillers generally run a little cheaper; however, the epoxy lasts a lot longer so the cost broadly balances out in the long term.

PAINT, PRIMER AND SPRAY CANS

Now that our model is built, we can start to paint it. Before we can look at some techniques, though, I should probably cover a few key types of paint and paint products on the market. Before this, though, it's best practice to give your models a wash in warm soapy water to remove any release agents – dust, finger grease, etc. – that can build up on the model and potentially harm the finish.

All of the following guides in this book will be for painting over primed figures, and for most of these I'll be using a grey primer as it's tough, hard-wearing and easy to see to work over.

First of all, primers are probably the most important type of paint you can get, especially when working with resin or metal. These differ from paint, being specially formulated to give a hard-wearing coat that gives a resilient surface for handling and painting. With most paints for

wargaming being water-based, this is especially important as repeated handling without a primer can cause paint to wear off a finished model. Primers typically come in black, white, grey and dark red, and I prefer to get them from places selling car body paints. If you have an airbrush, there is also a selection of good primers on the market for these. However, time and space constraints mean I'll be avoiding discussing airbrushes in this book.

When working with purely plastic models, you can get away with using coloured spray paints as the initial layer of colour. There are a great many of these on the market in both enamel and acrylic form, so finding something to suit your needs shouldn't be too hard. Notable ranges are the Army Painter, Plastic Soldier Company, Tamiya and Humbrol. When working with these sprays, I'd still suggest applying a light coating of primer and allowing this to dry thoroughly (at least twelve hours, although twenty-four is better) before applying the colour spray.

By far the most popular medium of paint used for wargaming is acrylic. These are water-soluble but quick-drying and hard-wearing. Most paint when purchased requires some thinning to get the best results, as paint that is too thick will not only be difficult to apply where you want it to go but it may also swamp the detail on your model. To thin your paint, simply apply a little paint to a pallet – an old tile or plastic lid is great for this – then add an equal amount of water and stir together using an old brush.

For best results, add a tiny amount of flow improver; this will hold the coverage of the paint together well while still keeping the paint controllable. It's hard to give any ratio of paint to water as it depends on the paints you have, the brands and even the colours used.

You may also encounter enamel paints. These are an oil-based product and, while useful, especially for basing and wreathing applications on vehicles, are of less use to us in getting our armies finished as the drying times are considerably longer than with acrylics. I do, however, like to use enamel washes during the basing stage and these will be covered further in the relevant chapter. The use of white spirit or odourless thinners is required for brush clean-up.

Paint brushes and care

As with most tools, brushes vary between super cheap where you get a pack of a dozen brushes for a few pounds, up to fine Kolinsky sable brushes that can seem hugely expensive in comparison. As someone who paints a huge number of models, I would say it's worth splashing out on the best quality brushes you can afford as not only will they last longer, they will work out cheaper in the long term. To illustrate this, I've had some expensive brushes that are used pretty much every day for long periods, and these are still very functional if now a bit worn. I also have a steady stream of cheaper brushes that seem to last a few months before being relegated to mixing and stirring purposes.

A high-quality brush will also give you better brush control and a finer finish. Personally I predominantly use the Winsor and Newton series 7, Rosemary and Co. and Broken Toad ranges. That said, for things like applying washes and dry brushing, I do find simple, cheap hobby brushes from the craft shop to be perfectly adequate. For less expensive though still serviceable brushes, Pro Arte, Army Painter and Games Workshop all produce useful types. Again, though, it's also worth having some cheap, disposable brushes for jobs like mixing paint, applying washes, dry brushing and applying glue; anything for which you do not want to use your best brushes.

Paint brushes themselves are typically made from either synthetic weave or natural hair. Synthetic brushes don't tend to hold paint as well as natural brushes; however, when working with acrylic paint this isn't too much of a hindrance as you will be cleaning the brush anyway thanks to the rapid drying times of the paint. Nevertheless, natural brushes tend to give you better control over the application of paint. Natural brushes are better at retaining their point for precision application and also hold more paint, giving the added benefit of being able to keep working on a subject for longer. Natural fibre bristles are at their best when used for detail work, especially painting areas such as faces or fine layered highlights.

As you work, you will naturally need to clean your brushes. When using most acrylic paints a simple pot of water will be sufficient for use between changing colours and to prevent paint drying in the bristles. Regardless of what your brush's bristles are made from, I'd not recommend leaving it any longer than a few minutes between giving it a quick swish around in some water. You can add a little washing-up liquid to your water too, though I've not found it necessary myself.

For more long-term care, there are a wide range of brush cleaners and conditioners on the market, and frequently there are products put out from each of the major paint ranges. It's worth investing in either some brush cleaner or better yet some brush soap to prevent excess wear or damage to your brushes' bristles. Odourless brush cleaner can be especially handy for aiding the restoration of brushes. Each of these products will have its own set of specific instructions, usually printed on the side of the packaging; this typically involves giving the brush a solid swishing around in the cleaner/soap, leaving it to stand for a bit and then rinsing clean and shaping. I've used a combination of brush soap and high-end sable brushes to keep the same fine brushes in use nearly every day for several years now!

With regard to what size and shape brush you should be getting, a size 0, size 1 and size 2 round should be sufficient. Though it may seem counter-intuitive, a brush with a good-quality point and fairly long bristles will be far more useful and give a much better result than a tiny size 000 for the vast majority of painting work.

You'll probably spot in the painting guides the use of flat brushes, and these are just what they sound like: flat, chisel-like brushes. These are great for using for dry brushing as they have a good amount of control and lend themselves well to pulling over the raised detail, allowing you to have fairly precise highlights quickly. They aren't compulsory for dry brushing, but do make life a lot easier.

PAINTING TECHNIQUES

Over the course of the painting guides, I'll be referring to several techniques. Rather than repeat myself in each guide, I'll cover a few of the basic ones here and then they are ready for you to add to your toolbox.

Dry brushing

Dry brushing is, as the name implies, the technique of using a small amount of paint on a dry brush to build up layers of colour by quickly flicking the brush over the surface of the model. This will have the effect of adding a contrasting colour to raised areas while leaving the remaining parts of the figure in shade.

While simple in concept, it can take a little practice to really become proficient with dry brushing. Foremost, one must endeavour to keep the brush dry, but not so much so that the paint becomes powdery or clumped.

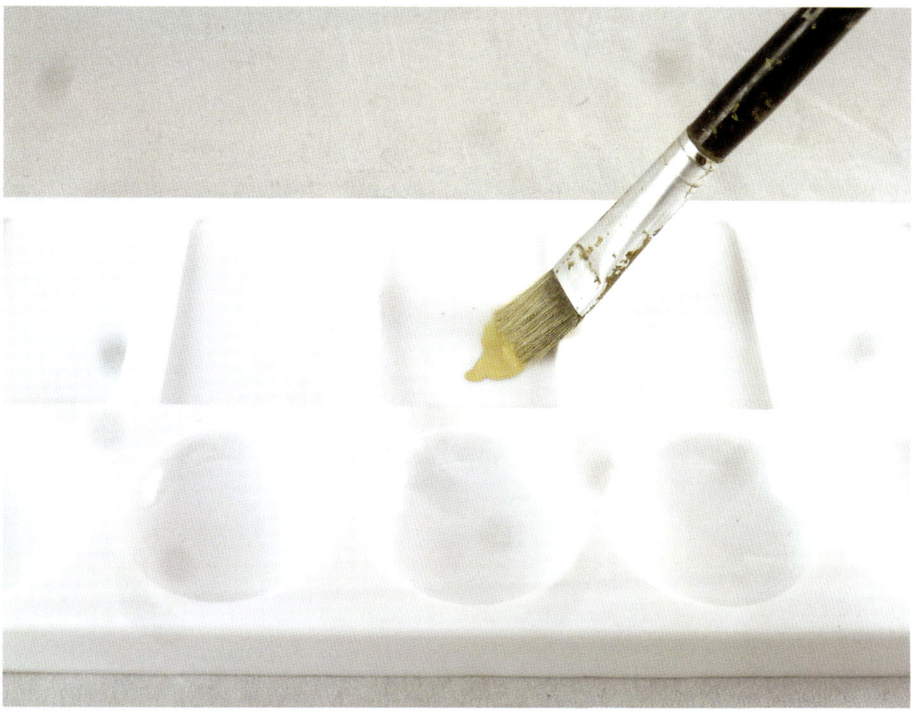

Once your paints are applied to the pallet, avoid thinning them and just load up the tip of the brush with a tiny amount of paint. Clean this paint from the brush with some tissues, then test to see how much paint is present by lightly dragging the bristles over some card or an old figure. You want the paint to be landing on the tops of creases, folds and details of the model, but also want to avoid streaking or blobbing of paint. With dry brushing it's best to allow several layers of paint to build up to achieve the effect you are aiming for as opposed to going in with one initial heavy dry brush as this can overwhelm your model.

One tool I've found to be very useful for dry brushing is the make-up blusher brush: they have soft bristles and allow paint to build up into very nice gradients of colour. These are probably of more use on 28mm figures than smaller ones though, to get the best out of them.

Layering

Layering (and edge highlighting) is a somewhat labour-intensive way of adding highlights and shade to our figures, and essentially is simply the process of painting in contrasting colours to create the illusion of depth and shade. You'll need to thin your paint a little more than you would usually; it's hard to give a precise mix of ratios, but by eyeballing it you want something fairly thin but that equally won't flood the model.

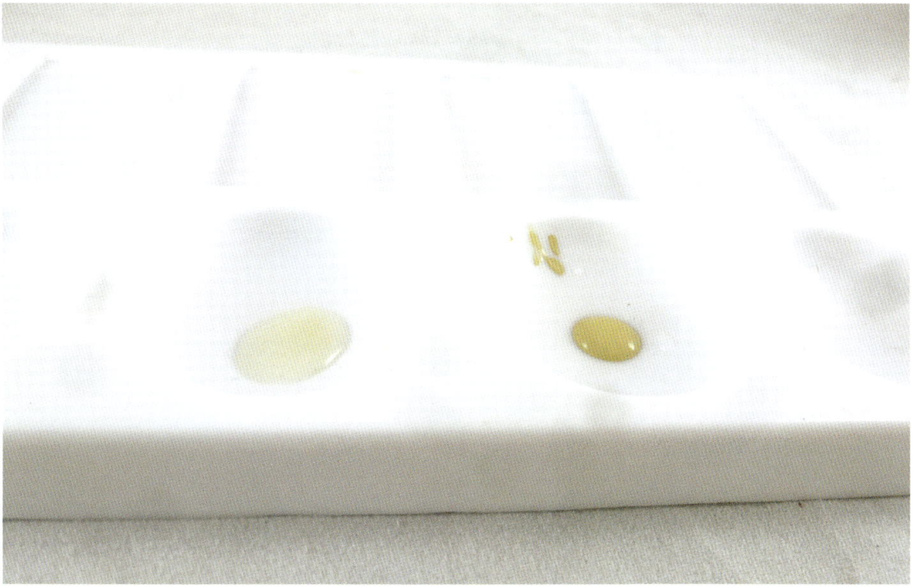

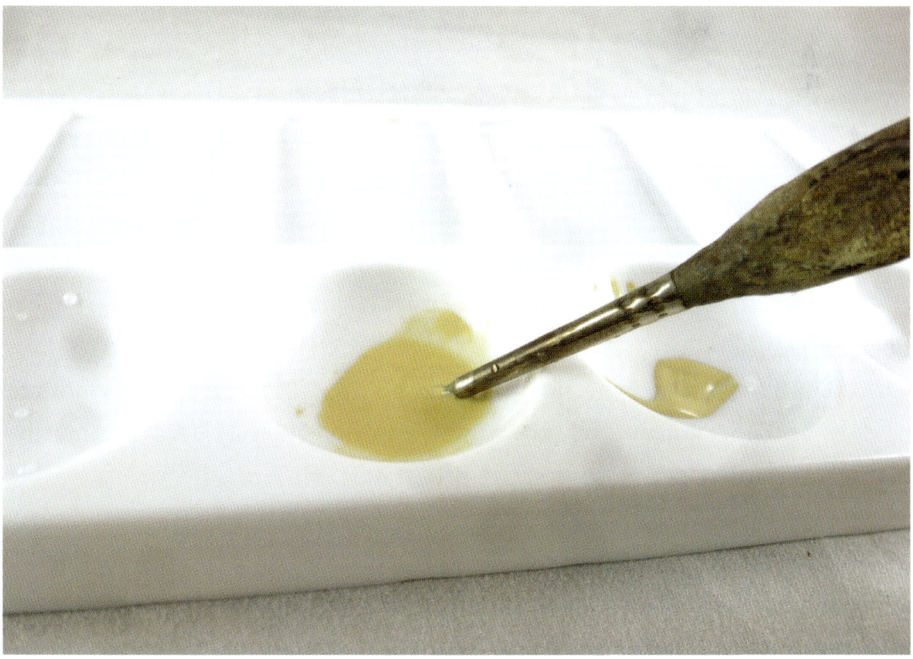

You need enough paint on the brush for it to flow smoothly from the brush, though not so much that it spills and floods once you apply it to the figure's surface. You'll be applying the paint to anywhere on the model that catches the light, such as edges of creases, hems of garments, tips of cheeks and noses, etc. To get the most natural look, pick a direction for the light to be directed from and use this to guide where your highlights or shadows land.

For more eye-catching highlights, keep applying increasing amounts of ever-lighter highlights to the model, applying the highlight to only the highest and most prominent areas of detail.

Washing and glazing

A wash is a heavily-thinned paint applied to a model that flows and settles into the details. These can be purchased as ready-mixed forms or you can make your own. To make your own, simply add two or three parts of water with a little washing-up liquid or flow improver to one part paint, and then mix these together. Paint this solution over the figure and allow it to accumulate in recesses and details, though equally try not to allow the wash to pool. This can be caused by too much wash being applied and thus flooding the model. A wash is best applied with an older though still well-shaped brush with soft bristles.

A glaze or filter is a similar technique to a wash, and is used to unify the highlights and shades already applied. The process is largely the same as applying a wash; however, it is applied far more sparingly. For applying a glaze, simply use a less heavily-loaded brush than you would a wash and paint this over the model, allowing the colour of the glaze to form on the figure but without flowing into the recesses as heavily as a wash would. This is a very subtle technique and is likely to be one of the last techniques you apply to a figure.

Varnish

A varnish is a clear protective layer applied to the model to protect the paint finish during handling. Varnishes are essentially gloss, matt or satin in finish. Gloss is very shiny, matt is very flat and satin is somewhere in between and largely depends on the manufacturer just where it falls between the two. Whether you use just one type of varnish, both types or none at all is entirely up to you.

Typically I choose not to varnish as it can have the effect of dulling the paint finish, although if you intend to do a lot of gaming with your figures, a layer of gloss followed by a layer of matt will serve you well as the gloss provides a tougher surface and the matt will then give a more realistic appearance to the finished model.

Varnishes can be obtained in many forms, but most useful for our purposes are those in spray cans. Such cans allow you to varnish many figures quickly and evenly, and also have the added bonus of generally being touch-dry reasonably quickly. Avoid spraying on hot or humid days, however, as this can cause the paint to cloud and potentially ruin your paint job! Brush-applied varnish will give you more control and is far less likely to cloud or have some adverse weather-related failing on your lovingly finished figure!

Hopefully these tips and techniques will have you feeling confident about getting on with assembling and painting your figures, and as ever should be treated as a stepping-off point for your own experiments. Now on to actually building your models!

ASSEMBLING FIGURES

So, with our tools collected and our miniatures sitting on the desk, it's time to start getting them ready for painting. With multipart figures becoming increasingly commonplace, it's handy to look at a few useful tips and tricks to enhance the assembly process.

While we've already covered tools pretty thoroughly and these should be all the ones you need, it's probably worth getting hold of some fine-grade wet and dry sandpaper too for cleaning up awkward shapes or particularly fine and light mould lines that may be too fine to require attacking with a file, especially when working with plastic figures. The figures used here are Warlord Games *Fallschirmjäger.*

While metal figures are usually single-piece models, or at most a separate head or limb, plastic figures, especially those in 28mm size, are frequently provided in multiple components. This can be surprisingly time-consuming and labour-intensive, and there is an inherent amount of potential frustration in working with so many components.

There are several steps to alleviate this, however. First of all, take the time to plan what you actually intend the figure to be used for. Will it be an individual figure? Will it be an officer as part of a command diorama, or will it be part of a rifle section of which you're trying to assemble many quickly? This will help you plan out the rest of the assembly process as it will guide you in visualizing the finished display. I highly recommend working in batches for this process too. My preference is to work in squads of eight to ten, though three to five is quite a manageable and handy number to work on too without burning out either.

Batches of this size mean that you can complete gluing a set of parts to one figure and then work through the group. By the time you are finished with the last, the first should be dry enough for you to do the next stage of assembly. I also recommend using these batches when painting too, as by the time you've painted the last figure in the group, the first should be dry enough for the next layer. More on this later.

Now that you know how many figures you need, firstly remove their bodies and, if separate, legs from the sprues, clean up any mould lines and stick these onto the models' bases. If you are using MDF or resin bases, you'll need to superglue the models to those bases.

When posing your figures, take a bit of time dry-fitting and playing around with the arms and bodies to see what sort of poses they create as some can work considerably better than others. A charging figure with a clearly aiming weapon will look a little awkward, while the same arms on a more static and careful figure will look far more natural.

Some figures may have separate rifles or other weapons. I find it best to fit the weapon to the dominant hand – typically the right hand – allow this to dry, and then allow this to guide the figure's pose.

Now the arms are on, it's simply a matter of attaching the figure's head. Again it's worth test-fitting the parts first as sometimes the neck may need a little trimming at the base to ensure the best possible fit. Although an easy task, the position of the head is pretty critical to the final appearance of the figure.

The head and face are pretty much always the focal point of a model, and as such need to be positioned in a way that is complimentary to the rest of the model. The aforementioned figure aiming its weapon will tell a very different narrative depending on the position and expression on

the face. A calm, quiet face will suit a more statically-posed model, while a shouting head will look better on a more dynamically-posed model.

The beauty of plastic models is that the number of poses and armament combinations possible from even a single box is simply staggering. The sheer variety of poses, however, is daunting and I highly recommend trying out some of the poses for yourself to see if they actually work and feel 'right', as it's all too easy coming up with something that looks spectacular until you find that an arm can't actually bend that way or there's now no room for the head to fit without some spectacular neck problems.

PAINTING GUIDES

Now that the basics of tools and preparation are covered, we can start to look at actually painting your models. The majority of these guides suggest painting over grey primer as this is my personal preference, though with the preponderance of coloured sprays on the market I really encourage you to experiment with using some of these. However, brighter, bolder colours can be harder to cover over, so it's worth bearing that in mind when debating using them.

All the models in the painting guides are from AB Miniatures, Eureka Miniatures, Wargames Foundry and Shellhole Scenics. Vehicles are from a variety of manufacturers including Hasegawa, Milicast, Plastic Soldier Company, MMS and Trumpeter. The majority of paints are from AK Interactive, Army Painter and Vallejo; however, you can use any range you wish as these are just my personal preferences.

I've broken the guides down by nation, and also split between the Waffen SS and Heer camouflage patterns. The models used in these guides are all 20mm size as this is what I use for my own collection, and it's also a good middle ground between the three main wargaming sizes: 15mm, 20mm and 28mm. The 20mm and 28mm techniques will be largely interchangeable. However, where relevant I'll note some steps that can be skipped when working with smaller sizes.

With so many scale models available that can work well with gaming, it seems useful to add a quick conversion table. Figure sizes aren't set in stone, however, and one manufacturer's 28mm might be quite different to another's, and even more so when taking into account heft and build of individual figures, so their relation to ratio scales is always a little problematic. This is therefore a more-or-less guide rather than exact. Some sizes have a bit of a range in scales associated with them. It's fine to mix them, but best to remain consistent as all 1/56 or all 1/48 with your 28mm figures will look far better than a combination of the two. Also, the lower the number in the ratio, the larger the model: e.g. 1/285 means that the subject is 285 times smaller than the real thing, while 1/56 means it is only 56 times smaller.

SCALE

Figure size	Ratio scale	Model railway scale
6mm	1/300-1/285	ZZ gauge
10mm	1/160-1/144	N gauge
15mm	1/100	TT gauge or HO gauge
20mm	1/76-1/72	OO gauge
28mm	1/56-1/48	O gauge
54mm	1/35-1/32	Gauge 1

2

Wehrmacht Uniforms: Most uniforms used by the German military and associated camouflage patterns

Feldgrau, or field grey in English, is a slightly misleading term used to describe a greyish-green tone used to dye the wool used by the Germans for uniform production in the Second World War. This is broadly speaking a green tone with varying degrees of greyness, depending on manufacturer and period. Later war uniforms made from recycled and poorer quality wool tended to have more of a brown or olive tinge to them by 1944–45.

Adopted in 1910 to replace the Prussian blue uniforms of the German unification era, the design and cut of the *Feldgrau* field uniform went through numerous iterations, and even from the start of the Second World War through to the end the design was gradually altered and simplified for mass production.

The simplest description of the German army tunic was a hip-length four-pocketed tunic with collar and epaulettes. Cinched at the waist, two pockets were mid-chest and two were hip-height. The details of the design did vary through the course of the war; however, earlier designs never totally disappeared.

The M36 pattern uniform, introduced pre-war and initially worn with stone-grey trousers, was the most elaborate of German uniforms with pleated pockets and dark green colour and shoulder boards. Simplification of this uniform was already under way before the war began, and was supplanted in 1940 by a new tunic replacing the dark green collar with a field grey one, the same as the rest of the tunic. Trousers were also manufactured in field grey from 1940, though the stone grey ones were still issued until stocks were depleted.

The tunic was gradually simplified, with details gradually being removed over the next few years, until the introduction of the M43 pattern uniform which retained the four pockets, though these were now simple squares. This would be the most prevalent uniform through the course of the rest of the war.

The final iteration of the German uniform was the M44 tunic; this only appears very late in the war but is often seen worn by the Hitler Youth and anti-aircraft crews. This tunic was very similar to the British battledress tunic, being cut off at the waist and losing the bottom two pockets.

Service caps were also made out of the field grey material. The peakless, wedge-shaped side cap was issued pre-war, and was largely replaced in 1943 by a peaked baseball cap-style garment, derived from the cap also worn by mountain troops. Officers and senior NCOs also had a leather peaked high-fronted cap. These visor caps have a distinctive band between the cap and top of the hat made out of a bottle-green wool.

Greatcoats followed a similar pattern to the tunic, being increasingly simplified as the war progressed. The pre-war M36 pattern featured a dark green collar and belted pleats at the back. By 1943 these had been simplified, and the bottle-green collar had given way to a larger field grey one for better protection from the elements.

From 1942, padded winter parkas and matching over-trousers were issued to combat the harsh Russian winters. Although later issued in a range of camouflage patterns, these useful clothes were also supplied in a mouse grey to the *Heer* or field grey for the Waffen SS.

Tank and assault gun crews wore their own variations of the field uniform, being issued a waist-length double-breasted tunic and boot-cut trousers. There were a few small detail differences, but the uniform was issued in black for panzer troops and field grey for crews of assault and self-propelled guns. Interestingly, the field grey double-breasted tunic was also trialled for panzer grenadiers, though largely in the Normandy campaign.

All the figures used over the next few guides are 20mm size and from the AB Miniatures range. While everything here will work well on 28mm and can be used on 15mm or smaller models, there are also a few stages that can be skipped with the smaller models. I'll comment on these when appropriate.

FIELD GREY UNIFORM

Probably the colour you'll be painting the most when working on German infantry, regardless of period, is field grey. There are dozens of potential methods, paint sets and formulae available, and I've tried a good few of them. The following is my current favourite combination of paints and techniques to get a good colour, and quickly too. My preference is to work roughly in squad-sized batches.

1. Dark grey base

To save time, I like to use a dark grey base all over the figure. This can then be used as the base colour for the figure's boots and webbing too, which can be somewhat time-consuming to come back and do later. Thin the paint so it has a nice flow and you may require two coats to get a solid base to work up from.

Brush used	Colour	Paint used
Size 1 round		AK3144 Dark Grey

2. Field grey mid-tone

The next stage is to apply a field grey colour. You can skip this step when working in 15mm or smaller if you wish; however, it does add a satisfying richness of colour to the figure.

I like to use a field grey that's pretty much halfway between being grey and green. This is our dominant colour on the figure and will be applied all over the areas of uniform. I quite like it as a colour for items of field gear too, such as bread bags, gaiters, helmets and gas masks or mess tins. Ensure you leave some of the dark grey base showing in the areas of shade, and also on the straps of the figure's webbing. If you find the field grey is looking a little dark still, you can go back over once the first layer has dried and either apply a second layer over the previous, or be a little more selective and apply the field grey to the more prominent areas of detail that would naturally catch the light, such as the tops of folds in cloth, tops of legs and arms, and so on.

Brush used	Colour	Paint used
Size 1 round		AK3141 Field Grey Base

3. First highlight

Highlighting will start to make your figure really pop and bring a great deal of contrast into it. I'm using a pale greenish-grey colour, but you could use a pale grey too. I like to have the paint quite thin and flowing nicely from the brush. Carefully apply this to all the raised areas, such as creases, pockets, collars, etc. If you want a more vibrant effect, apply a second layer.

Brush used	Colour	Paint used
Size 1 round	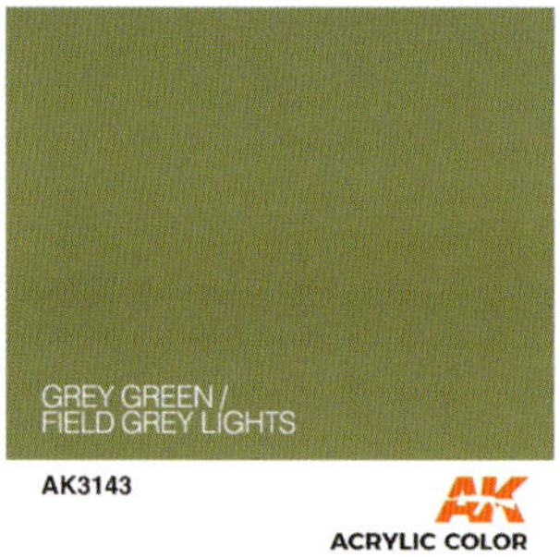	AK3143 Field Grey Lights

4. Filters

At this stage, your figure will be perfectly serviceable and you are free to go on and add the detailing and flesh tones. I like to take things a bit further, though; applying a filter and further highlight. The filter will act to unify all the previous stages and can also subtly shift the base colour.

While the differences are small, there is a noticeable shift towards the brown or green. Apply the filter all over the figure, though do not allow it to pool or flood the model. I've used two applications to make the effect stronger, and also used both colours. The tunic has had the green glaze applied, while I have used the brown over the trousers.

Brush used	Colour	Paint used
Size 2 round		AK3017 Green Glaze or AK3019 Dark Brown Glaze

Wehrmacht Uniforms: Most uniforms used by the German military

5. Final highlight

With the filter dry, I like to go back with the highlight colour and apply some fine highlights in the most prominent and light-catching areas of the model, just to further accentuate the details. With that, you're ready to move on to finishing off the figure.

Brush used	Colour	Paint used
Size 1 round		AK3143 Field Grey Lights

6. Early tunic and greatcoat

If you're painting a figure in an early-war M36 pattern tunic, using the greener tones and green glaze will suit you best. However, there is a further detail that will need picking out. This also applies to figures wearing the earlier M36 pattern greatcoat too. You'll need to paint the shoulder boards and collar a dark green. The easiest and most efficient way of doing this, I've found, is to use a green ink once the rest of the model is painted, and apply to the relevant parts of the figure.

I have also picked out the figure's shoulder boards with the figure's branch of service – in this case white for infantry – and picked out his collar insignia.

Brush used	Colour	Paint used
Size 1 round		Vallejo Game Colour 089 Green Ink

MOUSE GREY REVERSIBLE WINTER CLOTHING

1. Dark grey base

For painting the mouse grey parkas used by both the *Heer* and the Waffen SS, I like to use a pale but warm grey colour. This will be largely similar to field grey; however, there are a few subtle differences, such as the use of grey paint. As the figure still has the usual panoply of field gear and it's a nice colour to work up from, we'll give him a base of dark grey again and ensure that the whole figure is covered.

Brush used	Colour	Paint used
Size 1 round		AK3144 Dark Grey

2. Medium grey layer

I still like to use a fairly neutral medium grey colour here, one with more of a grey tone to it than field grey. With 15mm figures again, you can skip this stage if you're in a hurry. I only leave the dark grey showing in the darkest of recesses here, such as collars, armpits and so on.

Brush used	Colour	Paint used
Size 1 round		AK3145 Medium Grey

3. First Highlight

This step actually brings in the pale grey colour for the parka. I like to apply this in two layers: the first is quite thin, and leaves a little of the field grey base in the darkest of the recesses. The second I paint on as a broad highlight, applied to all of the raised areas to add some extra vibrancy to the grey.

Brush used	Colour	Paint used
Size 1 round		AK3146 Grey Blue

4. Reversible white

As the parkas were designed to have a white side for use in snow conditions, parts of this would show through depending on just how the wearer was using the garment. Often you can see the white at the turnback at the collar and at the hood. This will be very simple, and will just be picked out in white at this stage. If you want your figure's helmet to have a winter white wash, now is a good time to apply this too. Simply apply a quick, fairly rough layer of paint over the dark base.

Brush used	Colour	Paint used
Size 1 round		AK3027 White

5. Filter

As with the field grey, a filter layer will serve to unify the colours we've applied so far. However, it will also make the grey shift from being quite a cold, blue-tinged colour to a warmer brown tinge. I'd recommend at least two layers of filter, maybe even three depending on how dirty and worn-looking you'd like your figure to appear. This is applied all over the figure's parka, and padded trousers too if they are wearing them.

Brush used	Colour	Paint used
Size 2 round		AK3019 Dark Brown Glaze

6. Final highlight

To get the figure looking a little more grey, we can now add a final highlight to it. If you choose, you can skip this if you're happy with it as is. Apply the highlight colour to the most prominent areas, and here I've also applied a slight highlight to the white areas too, using more white.

Brush used	Colour	Paint used
Size 1 round		AK3146 Grey Blue

Wehrmacht Uniforms: Most uniforms used by the German military

PANZER BLACK UNIFORM

1. Dark grey base

The double-breasted short tunic worn by German tank and armoured car crews is relatively quick and easy to paint but adds a lot of interest to your vehicle models. Black can be tricky to paint, as too stark a highlight can wash out the figure or stop it even appearing grey at all.

I like to start my black uniforms with a dark grey base. This is the same dark grey we've been using with both the field grey and mouse grey uniforms. Apply this to the whole figure, ensuring that the paint covers smoothly and evenly, using two layers if necessary.

Brush used	Colour	Paint used
Size 1 round		AK3144 Dark Grey

2. Mid-grey highlight

When highlighting black, it is important to be sparing with your highlights. I try to confine them to the most prominent details, and areas such as the tops of shoulders and caps. I also use the paint quite heavily thinned as this gives more control of the colour build-up, and will use two to three layers to get the tone I want. For this figure, I've used a fairly mid-grey colour.

Brush used	Colour	Paint used
Size 1 round		AK3145 Medium Grey

Wehrmacht Uniforms: Most uniforms used by the German military

3. Brown filter

With a 15mm figure, this can be a good point to end painting the uniform and move on to finishing off the rest of its details. For larger models especially, though, I like to add a brown filter. This serves to warm up the grey tones and also adds more depth to the figure's colour, making it appear both darker and the shadows deeper. I'll usually apply two coats of filter at this stage.

Brush used	Colour	Paint used
Size 2 round		AK3019 Dark Brown Glaze

4. Second highlight

At this point, I'll add some very careful highlights using a pale grey, confined to the most prominent details and hardest edges of the figure's clothing folds. Be very sparing with this step as you don't want to add too much grey and lose the effect of the black uniform.

Brush used	Colour	Paint used
Size 1 round		AK3146 Grey Blue

GERMAN ARMY AND LUFTWAFFE CAMOUFLAGE UNIFORMS

The Germans used a bewildering array of camouflage garments and equipment, and even had a staggeringly wide range of camouflage patterns. I've largely broken these into Waffen SS and *Heer* (army) patterns in this book. However, the Luftwaffe (Air Force) also had its own variations, most notably worn by the *Fallschirmjäger* and field divisions.

The first camouflage pattern to be adopted by the German military was the *Heeres-Splittermuster 31*, commonly known in English as 'splinter pattern'. This pattern is very reminiscent of the dazzle camouflage used on warships in the First World War and features a light beige/grey/green base with angular patterns of mid-brown and green fairly evenly breaking up this base. Over this were printed the effect of dark green raindrops to further break up the outline of the garment.

The first item to be issued in this pattern was the *Zeltbahn 31*. This was an exceptionally flexible piece of equipment, designed to be used as both a tent and a poncho. Triangular in shape, with a hole roughly in the middle for the wearer to put their head through when worn, the *Zeltbahn* had buttons along the edge to allow it to be either buttoned together with other *Zeltbahn* to create anything ranging from a shelter for a few men to big command and medical tents, depending upon how many were available. When worn as a poncho, it could also be buttoned up to provide extra protection from the elements and also prevent it blowing around in windy conditions. The *Zeltbahn* had a grey-green base on one side and a browner grey on the other.

In early 1942 helmet covers (*Tarnhelmuberzug*) and smocks (*Tarnhemd*) began to be issued. From the winter of 1942/43 padded camouflage jackets and trouser suits (*Wintertarnanzug*) in the splinter pattern were issued. These were of a different cut to the similar items used by the Waffen SS. The *Heer* garments were simpler, the helmet cover held on with drawstrings and the smock lacking the elasticated cuffs and waist of the SS version. The SS smocks also had foliage loops on them. The most commonly issued items among the *Heer* were the winter padded suits, with the smocks being fairly rare and the helmet covers very rarely worn. All these items were essentially in the same disruptive pattern used on the *Zeltbahn*, with the reverse of the item left in white for use during snowy conditions.

The Luftwaffe developed its own form of *Splittermuster 31*, the colours used being the same as on the *Heer* patterns; however, the disruptive design itself was much tighter and smaller, giving a more intricate appearance. This began to be issued in limited numbers in 1941 as smocks for *Fallschirmjäger* as well as their helmet covers, and then in greater numbers from 1942 onwards. With the declining war situation, in late 1942 and through 1943 the Luftwaffe began to form field divisions, light infantry units formed from excess personnel and predominantly used in second-line roles. These troops wore standard Luftwaffe field blue uniforms, and many were issued a camouflage tunic in Luftwaffe *Splittermuster* camouflage material to wear over this.

In 1943 the Wehrmacht expanded their range of camouflage equipment, introducing the *Sumpfmuster 43* pattern, commonly known as 'tan and water' pattern or 'marsh pattern' in English. This pattern was similar to *Splittermuster 31*, though was generally but not exclusively printed with a sand-coloured base over which was printed a splinter pattern and over this a softer edge pattern, with the final part of the disruptive effect being provided by the raindrops effect. In 1944, the harder edge part of the pattern was deleted, giving the camouflage a fairly soft, tan-looking camouflage, very much reminiscent of the three-tone pattern used on German armour from 1943. Although rare, the grey-green base of the splinter pattern has also been used for the production of *Sumpfmuster.*

Tan and water camouflage was used to supplant the splinter pattern, though it never replaced it, nor were *Zeltbahn* or Luftwaffe field division smocks ever made from it. *Tarnhemd* smocks were produced, with a later pattern also being introduced that had a hood as part of the garment. *Wintertarnanzug* suits were issued from the winter of 1943, and *Fallschirmjäger* jump smocks were manufactured in tan and water from similar dates to the introduction of the rest of the garments. Helmet covers for standard German helmets are exceedingly rare in this pattern, were possibly only manufactured at a local level and do not seem to appear at all for *Fallschirmjäger* helmets.

SPLINTER PATTERN

1. Khaki base

When painting any camouflage pattern, there is always a balance between realism and something visible on the tabletop, as by its definition camouflage is designed to appear hard to spot. With this in mind, one must decide how much contrast one wants in their patterns:

you can use brighter colours to get an approximation of the scheme, or closer to the real thing for a more subtle but authentic feel. This is where I fall in how I like my patterns to look. Splinter pattern is especially notable for this, and with the complexity of the pattern and numerous colours, it can prove somewhat tricky to pull off.

However, there is a fairly logical process to the sequence of colour application. I enjoy painting more muted colours; however, if you want something a bit brighter or bolder, feel free to experiment.

To start with, the figure will need some light khaki base tone applied. If you are working in a smaller scale, such as 15mm or less, you can skip this step.

Brush used	Colour	Paint used
Size 1 round	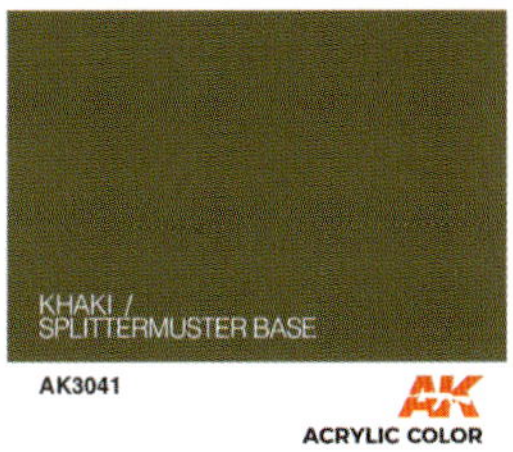	AK3041 Khaki

2. Beige highlight

While not wholly necessary, I like to add a highlight layer over the khaki. This is fairly broad and leaves the khaki in the areas of shade and recess. When working in smaller scales, it can be beneficial to treat this as the first layer of colour as the shade and highlights provided will largely be lost at anything other than a very close viewing.

Brush used	Colour	Paint used
Size 1 round		AK3045 Beige

3. Brown disruptive pattern

The main disruptive component of splinter pattern camouflage is a rich mid-brown colour. This is fairly jagged, but largely follows across a horizontal level and is formed of short, jagged lines. When painting figures from the Luftwaffe such as *Fallschirmjäger* or Luftwaffe field divisions, use a smaller, together pattern of the brown colour. For figures in the *Heer* such as this one, you are aiming to cover around a third of the garment in pattern. It is also important to leave enough space to add the green parts of the camouflage pattern.

Brush used	Colour	Paint used
Size 1 round		AK3031 Brown Leather

4. Green camouflage

The green areas of a splinter pattern garment are far less dominant than the brown and should cover around 25 per cent of the garment. The green should also be connected to the brown parts of the camouflage pattern as well. Where the brown component is made up of lines and angular shapes, the green areas are smaller and more like blobs, although the edges are still straight and angular. The green is a fairly medium green, with a bluer rather than browner tint.

Brush used	Colour	Paint used
Size 1 round		AK3025 Medium Green

5. Raindrops

This is very much an optional step and I'd probably avoid it with 15mm figures or smaller. It does add a fantastic level of detail though, and also is quite a notable part of the real camouflage pattern. The raindrops should also be applied in patches to maybe a quarter of the figure: using a dark grey-green paint, apply tiny vertical lines in patches to the model; naturally this will be most noticeable over areas of the beige base colour but will still be visible on the camouflage too. This step is tricky and it may be worth warming up first on an old figure or spare piece of card or plastic. The key is to keep the paint nice and thin and take your time. If you make a mistake, clean the area by lightly scrubbing it with a damp brush.

Brush used	Colour	Paint used
Size 0 round		AK3044 Faded Green

6. Filter

You may decide you want a more muted look to your pattern, especially if you feel that the various colours are looking too stark next to one another. For this, simply apply a filter or light wash. Either green or brown works, though I'd restrict it to only one light coating of either so as not to lose the camouflage pattern too much. On this figure I've used the brown filter on the jacket and green on the trousers.

Brush used	Colour	Paint used
Size 2 round		AK3017 Green Glaze or AK3019 Dark Brown Glaze

MARSH PATTERN

1. Tan base

While in some ways similar to splinter pattern, tan and water is far less intensive to paint as its disruptive colours have a soft edge and a smooth flow to them. While the guide here will be using the more common tan colour as a base, you could use the light khaki grey base colours from the splinter guide pattern if you were wishing to do an earlier version of this scheme. At this stage, apply a nice, even base colour of tan over the camouflage garment.

Brush used	Colour	Paint used
Size 1 round		AK3026 Tan

2. Light tan highlight

With a 15mm figure, this can be your base colour. I feel that this stage is more important than with the splinter pattern scheme, as not only is more of the base colour visible but it also serves to push the contrast with the camouflage colours, allowing a more pleasing appearance on the tabletop. Apply the light tan colour over most of the figure, leaving the tan base colour showing in folds, recesses and so on.

Brush used	Colour	Paint used
Size 1 round		AK3022 Orange Tan

3. Green disruptive camouflage

With green as the most dominant of the disruptive colours used in the marsh pattern camouflage, we'll apply this to around a third of the figure. This is a fairly medium green tone. Thin the paint so that it's fairly fluid and then apply it in a pattern of horizontal wavy lines. If the colour is not dense enough, apply a second layer, mostly in the centre of the camouflage pattern.

Brush used	Colour	Paint used
Size 1 round		AK3025 Medium Green

4. Brown disruptive camouflage

With the green pattern down, we can add in the brown colour. The brown is a fairly light colour with a reddish tone to it. This is applied in small blobs, and attached to the green areas of the camouflage pattern. As with the green colour, ensure that the brown is fairly thin and flows well from the brush.

Brush used	Colour	Paint used
Size 1 round		AK3073 Red Brown

5. Rain marks

The final optional stage of the camouflage pattern is to add some rain marks. These are a subtle but important part of the scheme; however, you can also afford to skip them if you don't wish to put yourself through painting them. Apply tiny vertical lines of a dark blue-green colour in swathes over the rest of the garment.

On the front of the figure I've used finer lines for the rain streaks and on the rear thicker lines to illustrate how they appear on the figure.

Brush used	Colour	Paint used
Size 0 round		AK3044 Faded Green

6. Brown filter

This is another optional stage and will mute down the previously applied colours, but will also serve to unify them as well. I like the appearance it provides of a more dulled down, in-scale appearance to the camouflage, but it does make it appear a little like a brown blob at a distance, so it's entirely down to personal choice at this stage. I recommend a brown over a green filter as this will add more warmth to the pattern.

Brush used	Colour	Paint used
Size 2 round		AK3019 Dark Brown Glaze

WHITE SNOW CAMOUFLAGE

1. Ochre base

White can be tricky to paint. I find that working with the darkest shade tone and then working up to pure white gives the best result. With white being a difficult colour to keep clean, after a fairly short time of wearing, the suits often take on something of a brown tint and we'll attempt to replicate that effect on our figure. With this figure, we'll be using an ochre base but you could use a mid-blue-grey instead if you wanted more of a pure white finish to the model. Apply the ochre all over the clothing of the figure you want to end up as white.

Brush used	Colour	Paint used
Size 1 round		AK3072 Ochre Khaki

2. Ivory mid highlight

On top of this ochre base, we will apply a thin layer of ivory or bone-coloured paint, though any off-white will do really. We will be applying this colour in two layers; the first will be applied over most of the figure's garment, leaving the ochre showing through in the recesses and deepest shades.

Once this has dried, apply a further, more selective highlight to the most prominent parts of the model such as the tops of arms and shoulders, tops of legs on kneeling figures, and so on.

Brush used	Colour	Paint used
Size 1 round	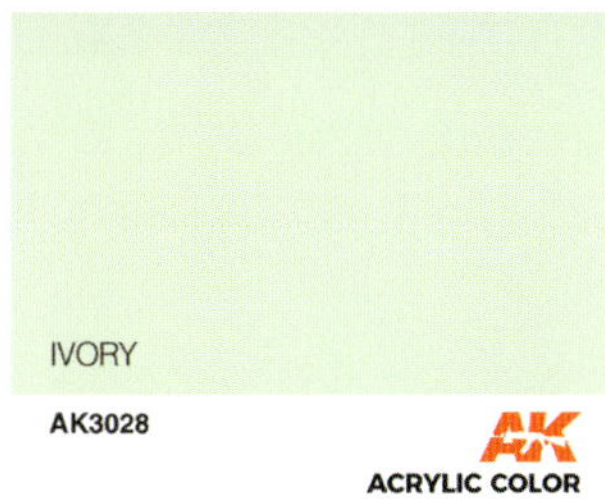	AK3028 Ivory

3. White highlight

At this stage, the figure is looking quite grubby and you may wish to leave it as is. To get a whiter and cleaner look, though, apply a white highlight to all the raised areas and details. You should find this makes the figure's detail really start to pop now. If your figure is wearing a reversible garment, now is also the time to pick out any areas of the alternative side of the item that may be visible.

Brush used	Colour	Paint used
Size 1 round		AK3027 White

4. Brown filter

While the figure is now serviceable and ready to go, I like to do a little more to make it really look more lifelike and used. The first stage of this is to add a brown filter. Depending on how worn you want your figure's uniform to appear, you can apply more than one layer of the filter. Here, I've used two layers to give a stronger brown tone.

Brush used	Colour	Paint used
Size 2 round		AK3019 Dark Brown Glaze

Wehrmacht Uniforms: Most uniforms used by the German military

5. Highlight

To finish the figure and restore the brightness of the white, I like to add a final level of white highlight. This is applied sparingly to the most prominent parts of the figure that would likely catch the light. With that, the white suit is done.

Brush used	Colour	Paint used
Size 1 round	WHITE AK3027 ACRYLIC COLOR	AK3027 White

3

Waffen SS: Camouflage patterns used by the Waffen SS

When it was first formed, *SS-Sturmbannführer* Brandt of the fledgling SS-VT pushed for the adoption of universal camouflage garments for the force. These were designed by Professor Schick. Where the patterns used by the *Heer* and the Luftwaffe included a series of angular patterns overlaid with a raindrop effect, those used by the SS featured a series of dots and blobs to create patterns replicating the effects of light and shade across a range of conditions and environments.

Initial requirements were issued in 1938 for a smock, helmet cover and *Zeltbahn* shelter quarter. These were designed to be reversible, with a predominantly brown side for use in autumn and winter and a predominantly green side for use in the spring and summer.

Both smock and helmet cover differed in design from those issued to the *Heer* in that the Waffen SS smocks were elasticated at the waist and cuff, and also later in the war, foliage loops added at the arms and shoulders. The Waffen SS helmet cover was also a more sophisticated design than that used by the *Heer*. The Waffen SS item had a series of clips and reinforcements that give a distinctive and visible pattern to the cloth. These also had foliage loops added later in the war. The loops are typically easily recognized as two or three strips of fabric across key areas of the garment.

Initially the Waffen SS camouflage was hand-printed and deliveries were slow. While it was intended that all Waffen SS infantry combat troops outside of vehicle crews should have a set, this was rarely achieved, especially early in the war. In 1940, however, roller-printing improved production speed massively, yet supply would still never meet the demand.

These items of equipment proved to be highly effective and very popular. Numerous variations of pattern were produced, but broadly speaking consisted of a light mid-brown base with two or three dark and light greens or browns printed over this as a disruptive scheme. Some schemes, such as the initial *SS-Platanenmuster*, featured a black-green or dark brown printed over a light green or orange-brown colour, while the later-issued and most common form of SS camouflage, the *SS-Eichenlaubmuster* or 'oak leaf', had the reverse, with the brighter colour printed over the darker.

With the success of the camouflage equipment, further items were introduced from 1942. These included peaked baseball-style caps, overalls, face masks and, from 1944, tank crew uniforms. From 1943 the padded winter suits began to be issued using Waffen SS camouflage patterns as well; most common of these were the *SS-Eichenlaubmuster* schemes, with the autumn brown scheme being the most prevalent of all. Unlike other SS camouflage garments, these were reversible to white rather than the opposite seasonal scheme, and were also available in field grey, mouse grey and, rarely, in the other camouflage patterns used by the Waffen SS.

The first pattern of camouflage to enter service with the Waffen SS was the *SS-Platanenmuster* or 'plane tree'. This was produced from the beginning of the war until around 1942, when it began to be supplanted although never replaced by newer designs. Several variations on the plane tree pattern exist. The *SS-Rauchtarnmuster*, or burred edge, was also widely produced. This scheme has an even softer and more blurred disruptive pattern and is intended to look like drifting smoke. The *SS-Palmenmuster*, or palm tree pattern, is yet another common variant, especially until around 1943. This features distinctive streaks of the dark colour in the pattern, giving the impression of the fronds on a palm leaf.

The final pattern of Waffen SS camouflage to enter service in serious numbers was the *SS-Erbsenmuster* pattern, or pea dot/dot 44 pattern. This was intended to be an all-season uniform planned to replace the previous system of smocks with a new field uniform consisting of tunic and trousers printed in the new pattern, cut in the same style as the M43 pattern field grey uniform, though worn with only a limited amount of insignia compared to the grey uniform. Just national eagles on the sleeve and low-visibility rank insignia were authorized.

Pea dot started to appear in units around mid-1944, but never replaced the existing patterns and garments. Pea dot was not used for the manufacture of *Zeltbahns*, caps or helmet covers; although some field-made examples may have existed, they would be exceedingly unusual. Jump smocks for *Fallschirmjäger* do appear to have been produced in pea dot, but do not appear to have been issued except maybe in ones and twos very late in the war.

The pea dot pattern is so named because of its distinctive appearance. Using a dark to mid-brown base, the pattern features blotches of pale green, black, green and tan, broken up with further dots of the same colours including the base tone.

While this covers the main camouflage patterns used by the Waffen SS during the Second World War, there were a few others. *Italienisches-Tarnmuster* used the Italian 1929 pattern camouflage to make several different types of garment including trousers, tunics, overalls and parkas. Predominantly seen in Normandy, the most commonly seen use on the Eastern Front was in fur-lined parkas. Despite the pattern being in Italian service since 1929, it does not appear in SS use until 1944.

Finally, the rarest pattern of uniform used is *SS-Leibermuster.* This was actually intended to replace all the camouflage uniforms of both currently in use with all the branches of the German military. In some ways, this was an evolution of the pea dot uniform and utilized the colours of the *Heer's* marsh pattern uniform with the rain marks replaced by black wavy lines. Interestingly, this uniform was designed to be hidden from infrared devices. Designed too late in the war to see mass issue, a few items have appeared in photos from right at the end of the war, and only in the form of M44 pattern waist-length tunic and trousers.

Before coming to the painting guides, it's worth taking a moment to point out that apart from a few rare exceptions, there isn't much in the way of swapping of camouflage between *Heer* and SS units. It's highly unusual to see *Heer* units with SS camouflage and vice versa, and even then it's typically restricted to individuals, usually officers.

With such a range of camouflage patterns in use, in these guides I'll restrict them to demonstrating the most common patterns: SS plane tree and oak leaf on smocks and pea dot on a figure wearing an M43 uniform. All figures are from AB Miniatures. There's not much you can skip when working in smaller sizes, but I'll point out the stages where they occur.

SS-PLATANENMUSTER OR PLANE TREE

1. Dark brown base

SS camouflage patterns look intimidating to paint and it can prove frustrating to get them looking right. However, essentially by roughly following the way the pattern was printed, they become relatively simple to paint once broken down. Plane tree has a brown base colour, so we'll start our figure in the same way, applying a dark earthy brown all over the figure's camouflage smock and helmet cover, using two coats if needed. While this is using the spring green camouflage, you can use the brown shades being used in the oak leaf guide for the autumn side of the plane tree-based patterns, substituting the light green for the light brown, etc.

Brush used	Colour	Paint used
Size 2 round		AK3061 Medium Red Brown

2. Mid-brown layer

If you are painting in 15mm, this can be your starting layer if you should wish to speed things along. Here we apply a broad highlight over most of the figure, leaving the previous layer confined to the deepest recesses of detail. You may need two thin layers to get the best opacity of colour here.

Brush used	Colour	Paint used
Size 1 round		AK3062 Cork Brown

3. Light green blobs

For the first stage in applying the disruptive pattern, we want to apply these to between half and one-third of the surface area of the figure's camouflage clothing, leaving room to apply the remaining stages of the figure's camouflage later. The green used is a fairly bright, almost lime green colour. You may find you require two coats to get a solid colour, depending on your brand of paint. However, if you are painting the burred edge pattern, then apply the paint a little thinner so that it is less opaque.

Brush used	Colour	Paint used
Size 0 round		AK3063 Golden Olive

4. Dark green blobs

Next up, we add the dark green component of the camouflage pattern. This is largely applied in much the same way as the light green, though a little bit more web-like, allowing the browns and greens to show through in places. Use a very dark green for this stage.

Brush used	Colour	Paint used
Size 0 round		AK3023 Dark Green

5. Dots

At this stage, we come to apply the dots part common to these schemes. We'll be using the light brown, light green and dark green in question and applying the brown dots first, then the light green and finally the dark green dots.

6. Glaze

You may wish to add a little more depth to your camouflage and add a glaze. While not necessary, it can give your figures a more lifelike and richer appearance. Once this has dried, you are free to go on and complete the rest of the details on the figure. If you feel this is too muted, go over a few of your light green dots again to brighten them up. It's important to be sparing here, though, and only do a few of them.

Brush used	Colour	Paint used
Size 2 round		AK30619 Dark Brown Glaze

SS-EICHENLAUBMUSTER OR OAK LEAF

1. Dark brown base

Oak leaf uses the same colours as plane tree and its variations, so you can use the following sequence to paint the green spring/summer version of the pattern. Here, though, we'll look at the colours used to paint the autumn/winter pattern of the garment. The brown base tone is a little darker and warmer than with the spring side, so we'll use a slightly darker brown as the base, applied all over.

Brush used	Colour	Paint used
Size 2 round		AK3053 Dark Brown

2. Brown-grey highlight

For the main base colour of the autumn pattern, apply a greyish mid-brown colour. We'll use this as a highlight, leaving some of the dark brown showing in the details and recesses, but we want the mid-brown to be a nice strong colour so be prepared for two applications if necessary.

Brush used	Colour	Paint used
Size 1 round		AK3051 Brown Grey

3. Black-brown camouflage

This is the first stage of our disruptive scheme over the figure. Apply a very dark, almost black brown over around half of the figure, using both irregular blobs and also small dots to build up the camouflage pattern.

Brush used	Colour	Paint used
Size 0 round		AK3056 Brown Black

4. Orange-brown camouflage

For this step, you'll need an orange-brown colour a little lighter than a mid-tone. Apply this over most of the dark brown blobs applied in the previous stage, and also a few but not all of the small black-brown dots.

Brush used	Colour	Paint used
Size 0 round		AK3054 Beige Brown

5. Golden dots

To finish the disruptive pattern, apply a few dots of a golden-yellow colour over the lighter layer. Be sparing with these, though, as you want that colour to be the dominant tone on the figure. To finish the pattern, apply some black-brown dots over the light areas of the disruptive scheme. Be sparing with these as a few go a long way to giving a convincing feel to the camouflage pattern.

Brush used	Colour	Paint used
Size 0 round		AK3052 Golden Flesh

6. Dark brown glaze

Finally, we can finish the figure off with a glaze of dark brown. As with the plane tree guide, if you feel that the figure appears too dark, go back over some though not all of the lightest part of your camouflage pattern to make it really pop.

Brush used	Colour	Paint used
Size 2 round		AK30619 Dark Brown Glaze

SS-ERBSENMUSTER OR PEA DOT 44

1. Earth brown base

As with all these SS camouflage patterns, we'll start with a dark brown base on the camouflage uniform this figure is wearing. Pea dot is a complex scheme, but broken down into its component parts it is fairly simple.

Brush used	Colour	Paint used
Size 2 round		AK3021 Chocolate Brown Base

2. Tan disruptive blobs

Unlike in the other Waffen SS camouflage patterns, we won't highlight the base brown. The camouflage pattern is so complex that this effect would confuse the appearance of the figure and make the camouflage scheme harder to see.

Apply a series of pale tan blobs to maybe a quarter of the figure's surface areas in rough, irregular shapes.

Brush used	Colour	Paint used
Size 1 round		AK3022 Orange Tan

3. Dark green blobs and dots

As with the irregular-shaped tan blobs, apply some very dark green blobs to around 25 per cent of the area of the figure's clothing. At this stage with the blobs in place, also apply some dots of the dark green colour over the rest of the figure's uniform. The dark green dots can also be placed over the tan blobs. Be careful when applying these as you don't want to overwhelm the effect of the figure. While the real camouflage had lots of very tight dots, this effect needs to be abstracted on a figure to have a looser pattern.

While I do not usually paint the field gear on figures with camouflage, this one has a rolled-up *Zeltbahn* I'm going to paint at this stage with a quick summer-green plane tree camouflage using the dark and light greens used here.

Brush used	Colour	Paint used
Size 1 or Size 0 round		AK3023 Dark Green

4. Tan dots

Apply a series of the same colour tan dots as you used in stage 2. They can be applied over the dark green blobs and again should be applied sparingly so as not to overwhelm the figure. I've also added a few extra dark green dots as there were a few gaps in the pattern I wasn't happy with.

Brush used	Colour	Paint used
Size 0 round		AK3022 Orange Tan

5. Light green dots

The final parts of the disruptive pattern of pea dot are pea-green dots. Apply these sparingly over the figure, with more of the light green dots over the dark green than the tan or brown parts of the figure.

Brush used	Colour	Paint used
Size 0 round		AK3024 Light Green

6. Dark brown glaze

If you feel that the camouflage is too bold and want to mute the colours a little or feel that they are somewhat jarring together, add a dark brown glaze as your final stage to unify everything. With that, your pea dot uniform is done. It's a challenging scheme to do, but looks great if you can get it right.

Brush used	Colour	Paint used
Size 2 round		AK30619 Dark Brown Glaze

4

Italy: Italian forces on the Eastern Front 1941–43

Italy entered the Second World War on the side of her ally Germany on 10 June 1940, sending troops across the Alps and into the Mediterranean. Despite the surrender of France two weeks later, Italian casualties would be huge, largely as a result of poor logistical support and bad planning; something that would overshadow the Italians' other campaigns, despite the bravery of their soldiers.

Following on from the invasion of France, Italian troops would go on to invade Greece and Yugoslavia, with Italian forces again demonstrating variable levels of efficiency. Despite having a large and, on paper, very powerful military, the Italians were hampered by a diabolical logistical system and further hindered by antiquated artillery and very dated, lightly-armed armoured vehicles. The vehicle situation did improve somewhat with some more capable tanks and self-propelled guns, though these were all outclassed by Russian vehicles.

When Germany began Operation BARBAROSSA in June 1941, the Italians immediately formed the *Corpo Spedzione Italiane Russia*. This corps consisted of 68,000 men and was formed around two motorized infantry divisions and a cavalry division and rounded out with various support and specialist troops. Suffering badly in the winter of 1941/42, Mussolini sent further troops to Russia in 1942, expanding into the Italian 8th Army.

The Italians fought in the southern sector of the Eastern Front. With the Russian breakthrough at Stalingrad at the beginning of 1943, the 8th Army was caught up in the collapse and largely destroyed as a fighting force. By the spring of 1943, the only Italian forces operational on the Eastern Front were engaged in anti-partisan operations.

The Italians fought a bloody war and took very heavy casualties, with around 50 per cent of their personnel killed or wounded and almost all their artillery and vehicles lost.

Italian troops deployed to Continental Europe and the Eastern Front wore a grey-green woollen uniform with grey-green straps and pouches, grey-green puttees on their lower legs and a grey-green helmet and black boots.

Adopted over a period of several years during the mid-1930s, the Italian army adopted a four-pocketed tunic fairly similar to the German garment, though in a greener tone. The tunic had wide lapels and collar, and until the introduction of the M1940 pattern tunic had a black collar. From 1940 this was replaced with the same grey-green as the rest of the tunic. Officers' tunics were of a very similar cut, but a lighter colour due to the finer grade wool than that of the enlisted men.

Trousers were baggy and didn't change in colour between 1940 and 1943, although they can appear a little lighter than the tunic through use and wear in the field. From ankle to knee, puttees were wrapped around the calf to just below the knee and these too were grey-green, though a greyer tone than the rest of the uniform.

The Italian army was poorly supplied with cold weather and camouflage clothing. Cold weather gear was limited to greatcoats in the same green-grey colour wool as the summer uniform. Despite Italy having had a camouflage printed material since the 1930s, no provision was made for a camouflage uniform beyond a shelter sheet/poncho that could be worn in poor weather.

White oversuits were used in limited numbers, however, predominantly by *Alpini* mountain troops and the elite *Bersaglieri* light infantry. When the *Corpo Spedzione Italiane Russia* was moving through Romania on its way to the Ukraine, General Messe purchased a supply of traditional Romanian winter fur hats, and these were supplemented by an Italian-produced garment when the force expanded to the Italian 8th Army.

Italian field equipment was also predominantly a mid to light grey leather colour, with water bottles being aluminium with a covering the same colour as the uniform. Packs and gas mask bags were a canvas or khaki colour.

ITALIAN INFANTRYMAN

1. Dark grey base

This figure is wearing the summer continental uniform and is only wearing light field gear. While similar to painting German uniforms, the colours used are somewhat lighter and will be subtly different. I'll also note painting of the figure's helmet and field gear.

The first stage is giving the figure a solid covering of dark grey.

Brush used	Colour	Paint used
Size 2 round		AK 3144 Field Grey Shadows

2. Green-grey layer

The first stage of highlighting is to apply a dark field grey colour. For this, you'll want one that has quite a strong green tone to it. Apply this over most of the figure, but do not apply it to the belts or puttees. Leave some of the dark grey showing in the deepest recesses. Apply this colour to the helmet too.

Brush used	Colour	Paint used
Size 1 round		AK3142 Field Grey Base 2

3. Grey belts

Before we go any further with highlighting the figure, we'll pick out the figure's belt and puttees using a medium grey colour. Leave a line of dark grey between these areas and the rest of the figure to create a deep shadow.

Brush used	Colour	Paint used
Size 1 round		AK3145 Medium Grey

4. Uniform highlights

To highlight the uniform, use a pale grey. Keep the paint quite thin and controlled, and if necessary build up the colour in two or more layers. This highlight isn't needed on the puttees or belt.

Brush used	Colour	Paint used
Size 1 round		AK3146 Grey Blue

5. Light grey-green highlight on puttees

This is a fairly tedious step but it does look good. You can if you wish, especially if you're working in a smaller scale, dry brush this colour on. Alternatively, if you want to show a little more detail, apply the light grey-green along the top of the puttee roll, leaving the grey base showing through in the recesses of the details.

Brush used	Colour	Paint used
Size 1 round		AK3143 Grey Green

6. Green filter

You can happily call the figure finished at this stage, go on to paint the weapons and skin and call it done. However, I like to add some more richness to the colour and apply a few layers of green as a filter to give the model a greener tone. Depending on the strength of the filter you are using, you may need to apply a few layers. I've used two here, applied all over the model. You could vary how many layers of filter throughout a squad or platoon to give a subtle variation in the uniforms.

Brush used	Colour	Paint used
Size 2 round		AK3017 Uniform definition filter green glaze

7. Final highlights

Once the filter has dried, the figure may look a little dull or you may want to improve the contrast between layers so that when viewed at distance the figure's details are more visible. This is entirely optional, however. Apply a fine and careful highlight to the highest points of your previously applied highlights. You can use this technique on the puttees too, using either the uniform or puttee highlight colour. Here I've used both colours to provide a great distinction. With that, the figure is finished.

Brush used	Colour	Paint used
Size 1 round		AK3146 Grey Blue

5

Romania: Romanian forces on the Eastern Front 1941–44

Romania entered the Second World War on the side of the Axis powers in late 1940. Despite a Western Allied-leaning political landscape, a combination of territorial encroachments as well as the fall of France led to Ion Antonescu deposing King Carol of Romania to become de facto leader of Romania.

Two weeks after the launch of Operation BARBAROSSA, the Romanian 4th Army launched Romania's offensive into Bessarabia in

the Southern Soviet Union, with the goal of reclaiming territory ceded in 1940. By the middle of July, Romania had achieved its war aims of reclaiming the lost territories.

At the request of the Germans, Romania pressed her advance into the Soviet Union proper, initially advancing on the port of Odessa in the Ukraine, which was eventually captured in October 1941 after a bloody siege.

Romania contributed the largest quantity of troops after Germany to the war on the Eastern Front, predominantly deployed on the Southern Front. By 1942, close to 400,000 Romanian troops were serving in the field armies. Probably the most notable campaign of the Romanians, however, was that at Stalingrad.

At Stalingrad, Romanian forces were charged with covering the flanks of the German forces investing the city. With the huge distances covered during the summer offensive of 1942, Romanian forces were terribly overstretched logistically and suffered from a lack of effective anti-tank weaponry and modern artillery. Armour support was also dated and not sufficient to tackle Russian vehicles.

Russian forces targeted the Romanians in their November counter-offensive, attacking to both the north and south of the city. Despite being under-equipped, Romanian forces succeeded in inflicting heavy losses on the Russians before being forced to withdraw, leaving some elements to be encircled along with the German 6th Army. Immediately prior to the Russian offensive, in November 1942 Romanian forces at Stalingrad numbered around 228,000 men. By January 1943 they had taken more than 155,000 casualties.

Romanian oilfields were to prove critical to the German war effort, and Romania would continue to provide large numbers of troops to the southern sector of the war against the Soviet Union, gradually being pushed back across the territorial gains of the previous three years. By the summer of 1944, Romanian forces were fighting on Romanian soil.

A combination of amphibious landings and sudden Russian mechanized assaults pressed deep into Romania, and despite fierce resistance from both German and Romanian forces, by August 1944 Romania was on the verge of falling. Antonescu was arrested by King Michael, who sued for peace immediately, with Romania then declaring war on Germany on 25 August 1944. Romania would go on to provide more than 500,000 men to the Allied war effort, fighting through Hungary and Czechoslovakia and ultimately being the fourth-largest contributor of troops to the Allied war effort.

The M1939 field uniform worn by Romanian troops fighting in the Second World War consisted of a woollen khaki-brown tunic, a peaked cap and trousers, worn with puttees and brown leather boots. Field gear consisted of brown leather straps, with light khaki-coloured bags and packs; frequently seen across the chest is an olive-green shelter or blanket roll. Although less common, longer marching boots in black leather similar to the German jack-boots were also worn, especially by officers.

In the summer, the wool tunic was frequently replaced by a cotton summer tunic that would bleach very quickly under the sun and appears very pale in photographs compared to the woollen trousers. Sometimes a yellow armband would be worn to distinguish Romanian forces from the somewhat similar-looking Soviet troops. These armbands would remain in use when fighting the Hungarians in 1944–45 as they too had a very similar uniform to the Romanians.

Until the late 1930s, Romanian forces had used a French-style Adrian helmet; however, in 1939 they adopted the Dutch helmet, which was painted a dark green colour. No camouflage patterns were used or issued; however, greatcoats of the same colour wool as the rest of the uniform were issued in the winter and white oversuits were also worn, especially by mountain troops.

ROMANIAN SUMMER UNIFORM

While this guide is for painting the Romanian summer uniform, for the wool tunic or figures wearing the greatcoat, the colours used on the trousers will work here too. The figure used is from Shellhole Scenics.

1. Dark brown base coat

Despite the figure being two-tone in colour, we will use the same base colour for both the tunic and trousers, and this will also be a good base for the webbing, boots and helmet. Because of this, you may need two or three thin coats to get a solid, even base for the rest of the layers.

Brush used	Colour	Paint used
Size 2 round		AK3074 Brown Olive Drab

2. Mid-brown highlight

Apply a mid-earth-brown highlight to the trousers. If you want your figure to be wearing the wool tunic, or if they are wearing a greatcoat or field cap, then apply this highlight to those too. If your figure has a knapsack, pack or water bottle, you can use this colour here too as their base colour.

Brush used	Colour	Paint used
Size 1 round		AK3081 British Uniform

3. Canvas-coloured layers and highlights

Using a light khaki colour, apply this to the most prominent, raised parts of the woollen areas of the figure's uniform. If your figure has puttees, paint the puttee strips with this, allowing the dark brown base layer to remain visible in the details and folds.

If your figure is wearing the summer tunic, apply the colour to the figure's tunic too, allowing the base brown to appear around areas of naturally deep shade and at the edges of belts and straps.

Brush used	Colour	Paint used
Size 1 round		AK3076 Canvas Tone

4. Light grey-green highlight

Given how much the summer tunic faded, you have quite a range of colours available, such as pale sands, light greens and light greys that you could use to highlight the garment. I've only gone for a little fading on this figure's tunic, using a light khaki colour. This is applied to any area that would naturally catch the light.

Brush used	Colour	Paint used
Size 1 round		AK3067 Deck Tan

5. Straps and field gear

With the uniform colours down, we can pick out the figure's equipment using a light sand colour to highlight any packs and water bottles and a reddish leather brown for the belts and rifle pouches. Sub-machine-gun ammunition pouches would be the same light sand as other canvas items.

At this stage, also paint the helmet with a dark green colour. As the figure has German-style boots, I've picked those out in dark grey.

Brush used	Colour	Paint used
Size 1 round		AK3072 Ochre
Size 1 round		AK3073 Red Brown
Size 1 round		AK3071 Dark Olive Green

6. Dark brown glaze

The figure is about done now, and especially at a small scale would be very ready to paint the flesh and weapons and call it finished. However, I like to take things a little further, adding some extra definition and highlights.

Apply a glaze of dark brown. I've only used one layer here, but if you want to add more contrast to the final figure, you can use two or more layers to build the intensity.

Brush used	Colour	Paint used
Size 2 round		AK3019 Dark Brown Glaze

7. Final highlights

We can now return to finish the figure, using the final highlight colours used in the previous steps to bring back the contrast between layers. However, we will be using a small brush and keeping the paint thin to make applying the highlights easier and more precise. If you wish, you can also add a yellow identification armband at this stage. With that, the figure is now ready to be finished with its weapons and skin painted.

Brush used	Colour	Paint used
Size 0 round		AK11047 Lemon Yellow

6

Hungary: Hungarian forces on the Eastern Front 1941–45

At the end of the First World War, Hungary had been forced to concede vast amounts of territory following the Treaty of Trianon. Hungary was led by its regent Nicholas Horthy, a former Austro-Hungarian admiral. This territorial encroachment fuelled a rise in nationalism that culminated in 1940 with Hungary joining Italy and Germany as one of the Axis powers.

Hungarian forces assisted in the Axis invasion of Yugoslavia in 1941, successfully gaining 11,500 square miles of Yugoslav territory; notably, Hungarian paratroops captured a pair of canal bridges during the operation. Throughout the rest of the war, Hungarian forces waged a bloody and brutal anti-partisan war in northern Yugoslavia.

Initially resistant to joining the attack on the Soviet Union, an apparent air-raid by Russian bombers gave Hungary the pretext to join the offensive. Hungarian forces assisted with the invasion of the Ukraine and southern Russia. Notably, the Hungarian Mobile Corps, along with the 16th Panzer Division, conducted a pivotal role in the encirclement of the Soviet forces at the Battle of Uman.

Through 1942 Hungarian forces formed part of the German Army Group B, operating in the southern Soviet Union. The Hungarians were assigned a 130-mile sector of the front and bore the brunt of the July Soviet counter-offensive containing it. They eventually managed to defeat this, albeit at the cost of more than 30,000 casualties.

Although not directly committed at Stalingrad, Hungarian forces provided flank protection at the River Don. By January 1943, the Soviet offensive turned on the Hungarians and in temperatures as low as -45°C fought a fighting retreat for over 100 miles. By February 1943, Hungarian forces had been withdrawn from front-line service, having sustained enormous casualties and losing most of their tanks, vehicles and heavy weapons.

Hungarian forces remained on occupation duties in occupied territories; however, they did not provide a front-line service again until 1944. From 1943 Horthy had sought an armistice with the Western Allies and had agreed to allow Allied bombers access to Hungarian airspace. This served to significantly sour diplomatic relations with Germany. This, in turn, culminated in the German occupation of Hungary in March 1944. Horthy remained head of state; however, pro-German elements were then installed in government positions.

With Soviet forces closing in on the Hungarian border, followed by Romania changing sides to join the Allies, Hungarian forces were mobilized again to defend their borders. In September 1944 Horthy again sought an armistice with the Soviets; however, the Germans got wind of the plan and SS Commandos led by Otto Skorzeny conducted an operation in Budapest that resulted in the capture of Horthy's son. Horthy was forced to abdicate, and in his stead Ferenc Szálasi, leader of the fascist Arrow Cross Party, became head of state.

Soviet and Romanian forces progressed further westward, eventually besieging Budapest in a three-month siege that would cost hundreds of thousands of lives on both sides. Fighting would continue to progress through Hungary and into Germany, with Soviet operations ending in April 1945, though Hungarian forces continued offering resistance to Germany and fought until the end of the war.

Hungarian forces were largely equipped with modern heavy weapons during the 1941–43 operations; however, by 1944 they were starting to receive German equipment to make up for shortfalls, especially in anti-tank capability.

Hungary adopted a field brown uniform in the 1920s. This uniform went through a few revisions but essentially remained much the same through the Second World War. The uniform featured a four-pocketed tunic and baggy trousers. Both the tunic and greatcoat were worn with a branch of service patch at the collar. The colour of this patch varied depending on the service of the wearer, but broadly speaking artillery troops wore red, infantry wore green and armour crews wore cornflower blue. Armour crews also wore a medium-blue set of overalls.

Boots and field gear were predominantly brown leather, though later in the war black boots were adopted. Helmets were similar to German ones and were painted a dark green colour. Canvas ammunition pouches and packs were a fairly light shade of ochre or canvas.

In winter conditions, the Hungarians had a winter white suit that could be worn for camouflage, and by 1944 had introduced a padded reversible suit similar to the German reversible suits. These were only issued in fairly small numbers, however. They were not produced in camouflage, but were a similar tone to the field brown uniform of the rest of the Hungarian uniform.

Hungarian paratroopers, at least up until 1941, wore a single-piece, light olive green set of overalls as their jump uniform, and this was also worn for parades and as a mark of their status. Other than that, their uniform was similar to that of the rest of the Hungarian army. Hungarian paratroopers also had a brown, sand and white camouflage smock, though this does not seem to be widespread in its issue.

The only other camouflage item produced by the Hungarians was a camouflage poncho, very similar to the Italian garment; however, this was not made into any officially issued clothing. That said, it does occasionally appear as privately-made items of clothing worn by officers.

The figures used here are all from the Shellhole Scenics range.

HUNGARIAN INFANTRY

1. Dark brown base coat

With the figure being predominantly in several different shades of brown, we will start with a dark brown base layer all over the figure. Keep the paint quite thin so as not to obscure any detail, and also ensure that you don't leave any gaps of primer showing.

Brush used	Colour	Paint used
Size 2 round		AK3074 Brown Olive Drab

2. Mid-brown highlight

Depending on how much of a green tint you want to your figure's uniform, you can use various shades of khaki for this layered highlight. I prefer to go for a pretty warm brown, however, when I paint Hungarians. For this, use a light mid-brown applied over pretty much all the raised areas of the figure, though leaving the dark brown base visible in the areas of shadow and shade.

Brush used	Colour	Paint used
Size 1 round		AK3075 US Field Drab

3. Canvas webbing

If your figure has a water bottle, bed roll, pack or similar items, pick those out now with a light khaki colour. However, be careful to leave a little of the dark brown base showing at the recesses and details.

Brush used	Colour	Paint used
Size 1 round		AK3076 Canvas Tone

4. Ochre highlight

To highlight the uniform and canvas webbing items, carefully apply some fine highlights to the most prominent areas. The idea with these is not to change the overall colour of the figure but to just create some visual interest when viewed.

Brush used	Colour	Paint used
Size 1 round		AK3072 Ochre

5. Straps and field gear

You can now round out the figure by painting the helmet and belt and webbing straps, as well as the boots. The helmet should be a dark green, and the belt and any supporting shoulder straps a leather brown. You can pick the boots out in either black or brown; I've gone for brown here as a change from the black normally worn by figures of the period.

Brush used	Colour	Paint used
Size 1 round	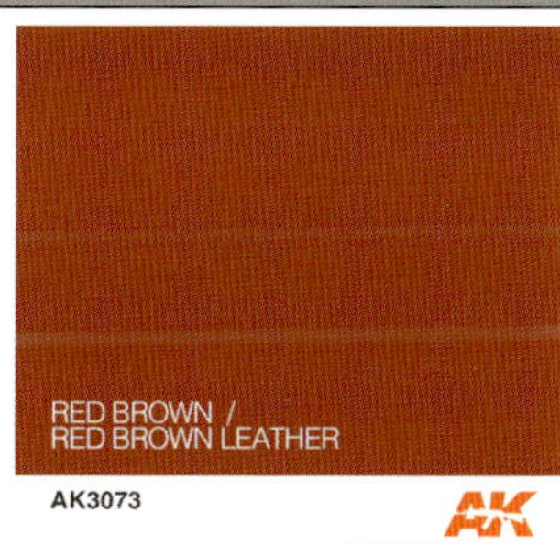	AK3073 Red Brown
Size 1 round		AK3071 Dark Olive Green

6. Green glaze

If you are aiming to get your figures down on the table and ready to play, the Hungarian is now good to go. However, if you want to invest a little more detail, you can add a filter.

At the moment, the figure is very brown-looking. While original Hungarian uniforms have a very strong brown component to their colour, they do also have a slight green tint to them. The easiest way to apply this is with a green filter. You may need several applications to shift the colour as far into green as you want to go. I've used two layers here, just enough to give the brown a shift to a slight green tone.

Brush used	Colour	Paint used
Size 2 round		AK3017 Uniform Definition Filter Green Glaze

7. Final highlights and collar details

Finally, apply a small, precise highlight to the most prominent areas of the figure's details and areas most likely to naturally catch the light, using the highlight colour used in step 4. If you wish to go the extra mile, you can pick out the figure's branch of service marking. As my figure will be from an infantry unit, I've used a grass green. With that, we can now finish his weapon and skin, and he's done.

Brush used	Colour	Paint used
Size 0 round		AK3025 Medium Green

7

Finland: Finnish forces 1939–45

While not one of the Axis powers, mention needs to be made of the important role of Finland on the Eastern Front. As part of the 1939 Molotov-Ribbentrop Pact, a non-aggression treaty between the Soviet Union and Nazi Germany, Finland fell under the Soviet area of influence.

In October 1939 the Soviet Union attempted to gain control of Finnish/ Soviet border territories. Diplomatic relations broke down in November after the Russian village of Mainila was shelled. Though later revealed as a false flag operation conducted by the Soviets, this was the pretext the Soviets needed to invade Finland.

The Winter War ran from 30 November 1939 until 13 March 1940, with Soviet forces advancing into northern Finland before being held at the

Mannerheim Line, a defensive series of fortifications built to prevent just such an invasion by the Soviet Union. While initially successful, the Red Army learned and restructured and finally managed to break the Mannerheim Line.

Over the three months of the war, casualties would be high on both sides but the Stalinist purges of the 1930s had stripped the Red Army of many of its most effective officers and the army took massive losses in both manpower and equipment.

After three months of war Finland was spent, having received no outside aid from other countries apart from a small handful of foreign volunteers and making do with largely outdated equipment. With diplomatic talks in March 1940 leading to an end to the war, Finland was forced to cede areas larger than the Soviets had originally demanded.

Finland needed military aid from a foreign power, and with Nazi Germany being so dominant in central Europe by 1940, no other nations were in a position to offer aid. Germany was keen to foster relations with Finland for the upcoming invasion of the Soviet Union and used Finland as a launching-point for the planned invasion in exchange for arms and equipment.

On 22 June 1941 Germany launched Operation BARBAROSSA, and a week later on 29 June Finland launched a series of offensives aimed at reclaiming the territories lost in the previous year. This would become known as the Continuation War. Great Britain declared war on Finland; however, the United States did not. The Finnish and German forces were largely successful in their operations, and the front largely remained static until 1944 when a large Soviet offensive pushed the Finnish and German forces back to near their 1941 start lines.

Germany supplied sizeable amounts of armour and weapons to the Finns, especially in 1944, and Finland also made significant use of captured Soviet equipment. With the success of the 1944 Soviet offensive, along with the rapidly deteriorating war situation for Germany, Finland negotiated a separate armistice with the Soviet Union in September 1944.

As a result of this armistice, German forces slowly began to withdraw from Finland; however, Finnish and German troops came into conflict in the north of Finland as German troops attempted to maintain control of both nickel mines and the Gulf of Finland. Pressure from Stalin led to the Finns launching attacks on German garrisons and launching the Lapland War. German forces would withdraw from Finland into Norway, but would conduct a scorched-earth operation as they went. Skirmishing with remaining German forces would continue into April 1945.

FINNISH UNIFORMS

The Finnish field uniform used all the way through the Second World War consisted of a woollen uniform in a colour very similar to the German field grey, worn with a peaked hat made from the same material. For summer use, a light grey tunic was issued and appears frequently in photos of the Continuation War particularly. Apart from winter white suits, the Finns did not use any disruptive camouflage clothing.

Field equipment consisted of a black leather belt with brown leather ammunition pouches. Water bottles had a grey wool cover, and packs were canvas. Helmets were either German-supplied, being of both First and Second World War patterns, or the Swedish M40 pattern. These were usually a dark grey-green colour. Sometimes these would be camouflaged with a tan overspray, and in the Continuation War occasionally had a skull and crossbones painted on the front.

For winter equipment, the Finns had a greatcoat of the same field grey wool as the field uniform. Frequently seen worn, especially in the Winter War, are various types of white smock, some worn long to cover a greatcoat. White covers were also available for the trousers. During the Winter War, equipment shortages saw civilian clothing worn too, with Laplander boots being very common and sheepskin-lined jackets being popular with officers. Fleece hats were also worn regularly in the winter.

When it comes to painting Finns, most of the colours have already been covered in Chapter 2, with the field grey being suitable for most uniforms and greatcoats, the mouse grey being suitable for the summer weight tunic and the white used for white overalls. However, with such potentially disparate colours together on a figure, it can be awkward to paint these in a time-efficient way, so that will be the focus of this guide. Figures used here are from the Eureka Miniatures 20mm range.

FINNISH WINTER UNIFORM

1. Dark grey base

Despite such a contrast in colours on the final figure, I still like to use a very dark grey base as the starting-point. This will also serve as a good base for the straps and boots, and also areas of shade around headgear and deepest recesses such as where arms meet bodies and the underside of greatcoats.

Brush used	Colour	Paint used
Size 2 round		AK3144 Field Grey

WHITE SNOW CAMOUFLAGE

2. Ochre base

Before painting the rest of the figure, I like to do the winter white areas of clothing. In this case, the figure has a white smock over his greatcoat.

First, apply a layer of ochre paint, being careful not to let the paint overrun into other areas of the figure such as its field equipment or trousers and greatcoat. We are using a fairly mid colour such as ochre as our base, as it will provide better coverage over the dark grey than some of the subsequent later colours and will also serve to make them appear warmer in tone. If you wanted a colder tone, you could use a light grey instead.

Brush used	Colour	Paint used
Size 1 round		AK3072 Ochre Khaki

3. Ivory mid highlight

Over the ochre, apply a thin layer of ivory. Try not to allow the paint to pool or run, but aim to keep it fairly thin so that the ochre still gives some tint to the finished colour. If you want to add a little more strength to the ivory layer, once the first coat has dried you can add a second, concentrating this on the raised areas. I have applied this stage in the photographs, but if you are in a hurry or working with a small scale, you don't need to.

Brush used	Colour	Paint used
Size 1 round		AK3028 Ivory

4. Final white highlight

Finally, it is time to add the white. Apply this to all the details and raised parts of the figure's garment. With the white areas of clothing taken care of, we can paint the rest of its uniform.

Brush used	Colour	Paint used
Size 1 round		AK3027 White

5. Field grey highlight

Now, add a light green-grey highlight to the field grey areas of uniform. When working on a garment such as a greatcoat, you will need to keep the paint fairly thin and apply a few layers to allow the paint to build up in colour density naturally. It sounds laborious, but once you try you will see that it's actually fairly quick to do and looks much better than a solid layer. At this stage, I've also used a light grey to pick out the figure's fur cap and scarf.

Brush used	Colour	Paint used
Size 1 round		AK3143 Field Grey Lights

6. Brown filter

With a 15mm or smaller figure, you could easily call the figure finished now. However, as this one is a larger size, I like to add a few more levels of finish. Apply a dark brown glaze all over the model. This will unify all the different colours you've used so far, deepen the shading and generally subtly bring everything together. If you want the figure to look grimier and more weathered, you can apply several layers; however, I've only used a single coat of filter here.

Brush used	Colour	Paint used
Size 2 round		AK3019 Dark Brown Glaze

7. Highlight

Finally, with a fine brush apply highlights of your lightest highlight colour to the most prominent and light-catching parts of the figure. Be fairly restrained with these, as the aim is to add further emphasis to the previously applied layers rather than adding whole new levels of highlight. With that, the figure is done.

Brush used	Colour	Paint used
Size 0 round		AK3027 White
Size 0 round	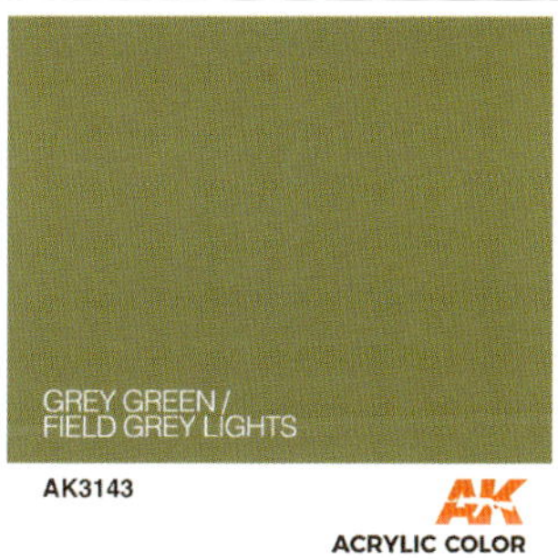	AK3143 Field Grey Lights

8

Skin: Tips for painting skin tones

The face and hands are hugely important areas of a figure to get looking right as they convey so much of a figure's narrative. Using a few simple colours and select use of washes and glazes, it is possible to add heavily to this narrative.

Equally, the simple use of a few well-chosen colours can get good-looking areas of skin onto a figure with only minimal investment in time and effort. Here, I'll provide two guides: one for a series of tanned skin types, and another for paler skin in the depths of winter. Each will have a simple start of a series of layered highlights, followed up with some select glazing.

With regard to when you should paint the skin, that's entirely a matter of personal taste. Some people like to work in sequence, starting with the skin first and then working out through a figure's layers of clothing; others by applying the most prominent colours first, and so on. I like to save the skin tones until last before basing, as the face especially sets the figure's character and personality, and I enjoy that aspect of finishing them by adding a certain spark of life to them.

All figures here are from the AB range.

TANNED SKIN TONES

1. Brown base layer

For a good, healthy-looking, outdoor Caucasian skin tone, you'll need a warm brown base colour, often referred to as either mahogany or flesh base, depending on the type of range you are using.

Apply this all over the areas of the figure's exposed skin, ensuring you do not go over the figure's helmet chin strap if they are wearing one. While not much of this colour will be visible, it's very important that the finish is smooth and even, so it may require a couple of coats depending on the brand of paint you use.

Brush used	Colour	Paint used
Size 1 round		AK3011 Base Flesh

2. Medium skin layer

Next up, we'll add what will be the main skin tone for the figure. I've used a fairly warm rose colour, and most paint ranges have something similar often referred to as something along the lines of a medium flesh tone.

Apply this layer over most of the skin, allowing the previous layer to show through in the deepest recesses such as the gaps between fingers, along the edge of the nose, eye sockets and so forth.

If you are working in a small scale and aiming to get your figures on the table, you could call it done at this stage and use them as they are.

Brush used	Colour	Paint used
Size 0 round		AK3012 Light Flesh

3. Light highlight layer

To add some further contrast to the model we will apply a fine highlight, concentrated on the chin, tops of cheeks, nose, knuckles and fingertips and anywhere else that may be catching the light.

This stage does require being quite precise and requires using fairly thin paint to maintain control. While I've used a paint specifically designed as a flesh highlight, you can use quite a few different colours; pale sand and ivory tones also work well for this step.

For quick paint jobs, this can be a good point at which to finish the figure.

Brush used	Colour	Paint used
Size 0 round		AK3013 Highlight Flesh

4. Flesh shade wash

I like to add a wash over the previous layers. This adds a bit more depth and richness to the colours used so far. There are quite a few available, of varying degrees of opacity. I like one that's a warm reddish-brown and fairly translucent.

Brush used	Paint used
Size 1 round	Army Painter Flesh Wash

5. Stubble and eyes

You may not wish to add these; however, eyes can add a nice detail to a model and really make it stand out, plus when viewed the viewer tends to naturally look at the model's eye, so a simple way to add them is to paint dark blue ink into them. I'm not a fan of adding whites to eyes, especially on figures of most of the average gaming sizes.

If you want to give the figure the feel of having been in combat for some time, you can also add a thin layer of blue ink over the figure's mouth and jaw area to give the impression of stubble. If you really want to give a feel of stress, you can paint a thin layer of red ink around their eyes too. I've done both to this figure. I've also added the red to the figure's lips as well.

Brush used	Paint used
Size 0 round	Army Painter Blue Tone Army Painter Red Tone

6. Final highlight

Depending on just how you want your figure to look, you can add a final highlight to it, applying a very careful and precise highlight to the nose, cheeks, chin and fingertips or pointing/trigger fingers.

Brush used	Colour	Paint used
Size 0 round		AK3013 Highlight Flesh

COLD SKIN

1. Brown-rose base

With such bitter winters and such long and important winter campaigns on the Eastern Front, you may want to collect a force themed to one of these operations. It's quite simple to convey the feelings of cold on your miniatures. First of all, apply a medium flesh colour; I've used the same brownish-rose tone that I've used as a base colour for the tanned skin.

Brush used	Colour	Paint used
Size 1 round		AK3012 Light Flesh

2. Pale flesh highlight

Next we will add a limited highlight of a pale flesh or ivory colour. Concentrate this on the most prominent areas: tops of cheeks, chins, fingers, etc. What we want to achieve is quite a high contrast between the main colour of the flesh and a few of the most prominent parts.

You can now call the figure's flesh areas done if you wish.

Brush used	Colour	Paint used
Size 0 round		AK3013 Highlight Flesh

3. Purple wash

To really sell the impression of the figure being cold, I like to use a colder-tone wash to a standard flesh wash. In this instance, I use a thin layer of purple wash applied all over the figure's skin. Apply this evenly so that it doesn't pool or streak, but so that it does tint the colours to a colder look.

Brush used	Paint used
Size 1 round	Army Painter Purple Tone

4. Red glaze

Similar to how we applied the stubble and stress marks to the figure with the tanned skin, these can also be used with the cold effect. We will make the figure's flesh appear flushed from cold. To do this, simply paint a thin layer of red ink over the figure's nose and cheeks.

Brush used	Paint used
Size 1 round	Army Painter Red Tone

5. Final highlight

Finally, you can now add a very precise highlight to the figure. Keep the paint very thin and very precise as you do not want to lose the effect of the previously applied glazes. You are attempting to reinforce the contrast between layers already applied as opposed to blending out the effects completely.

Brush used	Colour	Paint used
Size 0 round		AK3013 Highlight Flesh

9

Basing: Basing advice covering environments of the Eastern Front

The campaigns fought on the Eastern Front of the Second World War covered a staggering array of environmental conditions: from swamps to cities, to frozen plains and muddy villages, and temperatures ranging from 40°C in the summer to -45°C in the winter.

While it would be impossible to cover all the above in a book of this size, I'll look at covering urban bases and grassy bases and how they can be tailored to reflect different periods of the year, and finally winter bases.

Basing is one of the most important areas of finishing a figure as it occupies such a large proportion of the figure's volume when viewed and can really lift the finish of a model, even with a quick gaming-focused level of painting.

When finishing your figures, it's also worth painting the edge of your bases a suitable colour. Black is good as it serves as a smart frame to the figure, although it can also be quite jarring. Personally I like to use mid or dark browns, though I recommend experimenting and seeing what works best according to your tastes.

TEXTURING THE BASE

All of these bases will be created using the same basic texture. All will be working from a dark earth brown, with an ochre dry brush and then a selection of textures applied.

1. Brown texture paint

Apply an even layer of texture paint. You can put this on fairly thickly and then shape it to blend the tab the figure stands on into the base if it has one. You'll need a brush with a reasonable bit of shape to it, but don't use your best brush as with significant use applying texture paint will ruin the brush thanks to the microbeads in the paint.

If you are aiming to go for more of a summer, arid feel to the base, you could use a lighter, sandier texture paint and paler sand dry brush colour.

Brush used	Paint used
Old rough	Vallejo 218 Dark Earth Texture

2. Ochre dry brush

Texture paint needs a fairly long drying time, at least a few hours, especially if you've applied a fairly thick layer. Once it has dried, however, you can add some more interest to the base. I often like to use an enamel wash of a light brown pigment; however, for this base I've kept things simple and used a dry brush of ochre paint.

Brush used	Colour	Paint used
Size 2 angled		AK3072 Ochre

GRASS BASE

The majority of gaming tables and mats have a grassy, countryside theme to them, so matching that makes sense for most basing themes. There are lots and lots of ways to create a grass base.

The most popular ways involve applying a texture layer to a base and then adding clumps of either static grass or flock to it. Traditionally, the figure would be attached to the base and then have a layer of sand glued to the base, which would then be painted and dry brushed to bring in some texture. This does work well; however, I like to use a texture paint to achieve the same ends.

1. Dark green clump foliage

With all bases, I like to have an array of textures and colours to add more visual interest. With a grass base, adding a darker green clump of foliage adds the impression of uneven ground and small dense areas of undergrowth. To attach the clumps, simply paint a pool of PVA glue onto the base, pick up a pile with tweezers and place them onto the base.

2. Flowers and shrubs

Adding flowers and/or shrubs can also add some interesting texture to a base, especially if you're using the base for something larger such as an artillery piece. I've added a few different heights of tuft to this base and some flowers in small areas. It's important to pay attention to where the figures and models are positioned on the base as it's easy to get carried away and start to obscure them behind the foliage.

Another aspect to be mindful of is that when working in 15mm or smaller size you don't completely overwhelm the figures you have painted.

Attach the plants by applying a pool of PVA to the base roughly where you wish to position them and then apply the plants with tweezers.

When in place, if you decide it doesn't work, you can easily lift the plants off again as PVA has a fairly long drying time.

3. Static grass

To add some actual grass to the base, first apply some PVA to the areas where you wish to place the grass. I like to use two different lengths of static grass and two different colours. For a spring-themed base, you could use two different greens: a shorter bright green and a longer dark green. For an arid summer effect, you can use brownish-greens and straw-coloured grass. With winter and autumnal bases, use brown and straw-coloured grasses.

For this base, I'm aiming to create a spring theme so will use the shorter, fresh grass and a longer darker green as a final contrast to the other textures and plants.

RUBBLE BASE

With so much fighting of the Second World War taking place in urban environments, it can be tempting to use this as a theme for a force's bases, especially with so much potential for extra detailing. Larger bases give you the opportunity to add items such as furniture or architectural features especially. Here, though, we will just do a simple base of rubble and a few wooden beams.

This base will be created using the same basic textures already covered, with various grades of rubble added. For this base we will need a few grades of gravel and fine stones. These are all readily available from model railway scenic providers.

1. Coarse gravel

When creating a rubble base, you will want to use some larger areas of rock and then apply a finer gravel over the top. To add further visual interest, adding an organic element such as some tufts of grass or broken roof beams can add some extra features.

Much as with the grass base, apply some PVA glue to the base and then add some larger areas of the coarse gravel.

2. Organic debris

Here I'm using some finely-chopped pieces of wood made out of a coffee stirrer and stained with dark brown and black paints fairly roughly to appear burned and weathered.

While the PVA from Step 1 is still wet, apply a few lengths of the wood to the base, doing your best to position them in a way that is complementary to the figure without obscuring it. Alternatively, you may wish to add some tufts of grass or plants to the base. Once placed, allow to dry before progressing to the next step.

3. Fine gravel

With the larger components of the base added, you can now apply some fine gravel to simulate rubble. I like to use a few different colours and consistencies poured into a tub and then sprinkle a pinch of it over the base after applying PVA to the areas where I want it to fit. You could now call the base done; however, there are a few stages I like to do once the PVA is fully hardened to really bring the base to life.

4. Dark brown wash

When every part of the model is painted, adding something that isn't painted, such as the rubble we've added to the base, can be a little jarring to the eye as you view the model. This is quite simple to address, but can make a big difference to the appearance of the base.

With the previous stages dry, apply a dark brown wash to the base. Alternatively, you could use a light grey to give a dusty effect. I've chosen the dark brown as it will complement the tones of the figure and frame it nicely. Apply the wash all over the base.

Brush used	Paint used
Old rough	Army Painter Dark Tone

5. Light grey dry brush

If you wish, you can add some further contrast to the colours on the base by applying a light sand or pale grey dry brush. Ensure that this is only a fairly light dry brushing to enhance the details as you don't want to obscure too much of the texture and tones in the gravel. The base is now done. You may still choose to add further areas of grass or even detail items like old newspaper, but I like to keep the bases relatively simple.

Brush used	Colour	Paint used
Size 1 flat head		AK3146 Grey Blue

SNOW BASE

When one thinks of the war on the Eastern Front, the mind immediately springs to thoughts of battles in the winter and icy, snow-covered sieges. There are essentially two kinds of snow base one can make: one that is pretty much pure driven snow and the other patchy and partially thawed. The application of the snow effect for both here is the same; however, the base is slightly different.

For a pure snow base, simply paint the base a pale blue or pale grey colour and leave to dry. I shall demonstrate the effect on both the rubble base we created earlier, as well as a pale blue base. With either style, it is important to allow the base enough time for the paint and glues to fully harden. Due to time constraints between Steps 1 and 2, I've combined both stages in the accompanying images.

1. Applying water effect

With both these styles of snow base, we will be applying a layer of acrylic water-effect paste and then adding bicarbonate of soda to add the water effect. Simply paint it on fairly thickly to the required areas. For the pure snow look, apply a thick layer of water effect all over the base. For application over a base that has been detailed and textured, apply the water effect in patches to your chosen areas. The water effect is tough enough, yet light enough to be applied to long tufts of grass as well.

Brush used	Colour	Paint used
Size 2 round		Vallejo 201 Water Texture acrylic

2. Applying snow

While the water effect is still wet, apply your snow texture to the base. I like to use bicarbonate of soda, although there are a great many commercial products also available. The bicarbonate partially absorbs the water effect and becomes impregnated by the acrylic, so that once it dries it has a hardened surface yet also retains a bit of texture. Once you have applied your snow, leave the base to dry somewhere flat and the base is done.